PENGUIN ELEMENTARY
READING SKILLS

Anne Parry and Mark Bartram

PENGUIN BOOKS

PENGUIN BOOKS

Published by the Penguin Group
Penguin Books Ltd, 27 Wrights Lane, London W8 5TZ, England
Penguin Books USA Inc., 375 Hudson Street, New York, New York 10014, USA
Penguin Books Australia Ltd, Ringwood, Victoria, Australia
Penguin Books Canada Ltd, 10 Alcorn Avenue, Toronto, Ontario, Canada M4V 3B2
Penguin Books (NZ) Ltd, 182–190 Wairau Road, Auckland 10, New Zealand

Penguin Books Ltd, Registered Offices: Harmondsworth, Middlesex, England

First published 1989
10 9 8

Copyright © Mark Bartram and Anne Parry 1989
All rights reserved

Set in Linotron 202 Garamond

Made and printed in England by The Bath Press

Except in the United States of America, this book is sold subject
to the condition that it shall not, by way of trade or otherwise, be lent,
re-sold, hired out, or otherwise circulated without the publisher's
prior consent in any form of binding or cover other than that in which
it is published and without a similar condition including this condition
being imposed on the subsequent purchaser

Contents

Acknowledgements		4

Introduction
To the Student		5
To the Teacher		5

Section A
UNIT 1	Guessing Difficult Words (1)	8
UNIT 2	Predicting (1)	15
UNIT 3	Using a Monolingual (English–English) Dictionary (1)	22
UNIT 4	Finding Your Way Around a Text (1)	30
UNIT 5	Skimming and Scanning (1)	38
UNIT 6	Looking for Detailed Information (1)	46
UNIT 7	Mixed Skills (1)	55

Section B
UNIT 8	Guessing Difficult Words (2)	62
UNIT 9	Predicting (2)	71
UNIT 10	Using a Monolingual (English–English) Dictionary (2)	79
UNIT 11	Finding Your Way Around a Text (2)	84
UNIT 12	Skimming and Scanning (2)	94
UNIT 13	Looking for Detailed Information (2)	102
UNIT 14	Mixed Skills (2)	112

Teacher's Notes		121
Key		129

Acknowledgements

The authors and publishers are grateful to the following copyright owners for permission to reproduce texts, photographs and illustrations. Every endeavour has been made to contact copyright owners and apologies are expressed for any omissions.

p22–9, p79–83: from the *Longman Active Study Dictionary of English*, ed. Della Summers, Longman, 1983
p41: reproduced by permission of British Railways Board
p95: reproduced by permission of the Scottish Tourist Board, 23 Ravelston Terrace, Edinburgh EH4 3EU
p100–1: reproduced by permission of the *Daily Telegraph*
p103: reproduced by permission of the Scottish Tourist Board
p110: reproduced by permission of Pedigree Petfoods
p114: reproduced with kind permission of Consumers' Association

The authors would like to thank the following for their help in the writing of this book:
The staff and students of the Cambridge School, Verona, Italy; Joy McKellen; Michael Nation; H. A. Swan; Carla Ierimonte; Lorella Pagani.

Introduction

To the Student

This book will help you to read better in English. You can also use it to build up your knowledge of English grammar and vocabulary, but that is not its main function.

What does this mean?

Many students who read in a foreign language think that 'reading' means 'understanding and/or translating every word'. This is not so. Good readers do not always try to understand everything, especially the first time they read something. Much depends on the kind of passage they are reading, and why they are reading it. Sometimes they read quickly – to get a particular piece of information, for example. They do not worry when they see a difficult word; they try and guess what it means.

This book will help you to:
 (i) guess the meaning of difficult words in a piece of English (units 1, 8)
 (ii) predict what you are going to read (units 2, 9)
 (iii) use a monolingual dictionary (units 3, 10)
 (iv) find your way around a text (units 4, 11)
 (v) read texts quickly (units 5, 12)
 (vi) read in detail (units 6, 13)

The best way to get better at reading is to read. Don't worry if what you read is not 'serious' or 'important'. Read what you want to read. If you are interested in computers, read about computers; if you like cooking, read cookbooks! The important thing is to read as much as possible and to enjoy it.

To the Teacher

What is this book?

This book is designed to train elementary and lower-intermediate students to develop their ability to read English. Students who have completed an activity or read a passage in this book will not only have understood that passage, but will also have developed their capacity to understand any similar passage in English.

For this reason, the development of the students' knowledge of the grammar and vocabulary of English is not the principal aim. This, of course, is important, and will certainly help their reading – but it lies outside the scope of this book.

Who is it for?

The material is aimed at elementary and lower-intermediate students. Students starting at page 8 will have had at least 50 hours of study, while those who start at the beginning of section B will have studied for at least

100 hours. The book can be followed on its own, or integrated into a general English course.

How is the book organised?

The book is divided into two sections, A and B, each of which contains seven units. The first six units of each section concentrate on particular skills or reading strategies which the students need to develop in order to read more efficiently. These include guessing difficult vocabulary, scanning a text for a particular piece of information, and so on. The seventh and last unit of each section includes work on several skills at once, since it is uncommon for readers to use these skills in isolation.

Both the passages and the activities become progressively more difficult as the student works through the book: it is therefore advisable to start at unit 1 and work through to unit 7 and/or from unit 8 to unit 14. In particular, it is not advisable to work on units 7 and 14 (mixed skills) without having done the preceding units, since students will not know what is expected of them.

How do I plan a reading lesson?

Reading lessons need as much planning as any other lessons and what happens before and after the reading of the text is as important as the reading itself.

Before reading: the students must be given a reason to read. Students who are just handed a text and told to read it, without any preparation or motivation, will probably find it difficult and/or boring. The reason for reading can be:
  (i) because they are interested in the content of the passage. This interest might be aroused by an introductory discussion, by finding out the students' personal experience of the topic, or by giving the students a quiz about the subject

  AND/OR

  (ii) because the students have been given some kind of task to perform while they are reading. This might be a linguistic task ('Make a list of all the vocabulary you expect to find in the text, and then read it to see if you were right') or non-linguistic ('Draw a diagram based on the information in the text') or subjective/personal ('Does this text make you feel happy, sad or angry?'). Many of the activities in this book involve some kind of this 'task reading'. Other examples can be found in *Developing Reading Skills* by F. Grellet (Cambridge University Press).

After reading: equally important is the time you spend going over the answers afterwards. It will help the students if the class discusses which answers were correct, and how these answers were arrived at, rather than simply to be given a list of the correct answers without comment. In this way, the students will be able to transfer the skill to the next passage they read. This is particularly true with the units on vocabulary guessing and textual reference.

Should I pre-teach vocabulary?

For the activities in this book, pre-teaching of vocabulary should not be necessary. Most of the activities are designed either to encourage students to understand texts without worrying too much about the vocabulary or to guess the vocabulary from its form or context. Where the vocabulary is essential, and cannot be guessed, students should be encouraged to use a monolingual dictionary (see units 3 and 10). If the students get into the habit of expecting the teacher to explain difficult words, they will have problems later when the teacher is not present to help them.

What about reading aloud and translating?

Many teachers and researchers into reading believe that reading aloud is probably bad for students' reading abilities, because it forces them to read too slowly and concentrate on every word. Good readers tend to read quicker, and take in 'chunks' of a sentence at a time. (Reading aloud may be good for pronunciation, but that is another matter.)

Translating by students may test their understanding, but it does not train them to read better. Furthermore, it tests their understanding of each word equally, and does not allow for the fact that in any text some words can usually be ignored or skipped over.

The occasional translating of some individual words by the teacher (not by the students) is probably a useful, time-saving device, but it
   (i) deprives the students of useful exposure to English
   (ii) can only work where the mother-tongue has a close equivalent to the English word.

Any translation should be done after the activities in this book not before them.

Pair-work and Group-work

We suggest that you encourage students to complete the activities in this book in pairs or groups. This increases the co-operative atmosphere in the class, and it also allows weaker readers to see how the better readers work at the text, using all the resources at their disposal to extract the meaning.

Reading outside the classroom

Reading is one area where students can improve their English easily and enjoyably outside the class. What is more, it seems clear that the more you read, the better you read.

The problem is often that reading comes to be associated in the student's mind with just another way of practising English, rather than an enjoyable end in itself. For this reason, students should be encouraged to read as much as possible in English outside the class, but also they should be encouraged to read what they want to read. Too many people have been put off reading in English by being forced to read texts which were too heavy, too long, or largely irrelevant to them. By all means introduce your students to Shakespeare or Keats, but do not force them to read them. It may well be that material like pop magazines, romantic novels and song lyrics is of greater long-term benefit, because it provides an enjoyable introduction to reading English, which may lead on to 'worthier' things later.

Section A

UNIT 1

Guessing Difficult Words (1)

It is often difficult or impossible to use a dictionary when you are reading English – for example, on the bus, in an examination or on the beach. Sometimes the dictionary is too small or too old. So it is important to try and read as much as possible *without* a dictionary.

What can you do when you meet a word which you do not understand? You can:
(i) try to understand a word from its *context* (The context means the words and sentences before and after the word.)
(ii) try to understand the word from its *form*.

Understanding a word from its context

Activity 1.1

Look at the eight sentences. In each sentence, one word is in *italics* – in the first sentence, this word is *cello*. The eight words each correspond with one of the eight pictures. Can you match the word with the picture? The first one is done for you. NO DICTIONARIES!

1 She loves music: she can play the guitar, the piano and the *cello*. ___e___
2 He walked into the sitting-room and sat down on the *settee*. _____
3 Look! There's an enormous *fly* on the window. _____
4 Cricket is a game played with a small, hard ball, and a long, heavy *bat*. _____
5 A: Where shall we meet?
   B: Let's meet outside the *mosque* in Regent's Park. _____
6 He put the key and the *padlock* in his pocket. _____
7 Break two eggs into a *bowl*. _____
8 In Greece, you often see old women riding *donkeys*. _____

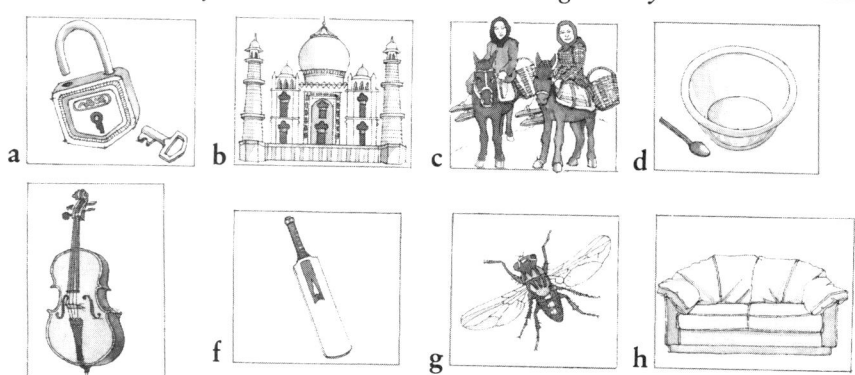

/8/

Activity 1.2

Match the word in *italics* in each sentence with one of the three pictures; a, b or c. Use the rest of the sentence to help you.

1 Mary lives in a small *cottage* in the country.

2 I usually go to work on a *scooter*.

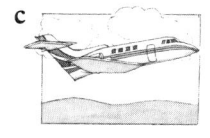

3 He was wearing pyjamas and a pair of old *slippers*.

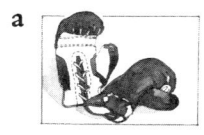

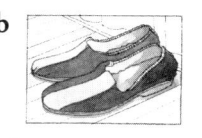

4 I'd like some *ink* for my pen, please.

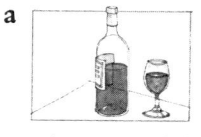

5 The *mast* of the boat was about 12 metres high.

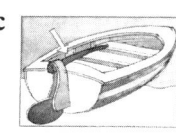

6 When I came in, the dog was lying on the *rug*.

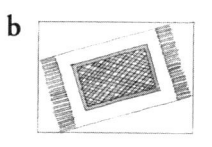

7 'Can I have *haddock*, new potatoes and peas, please?'

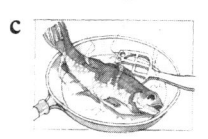

8 Hang your coat on the *peg*, please.

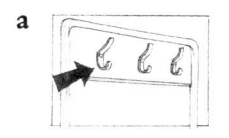

/9/

Activity 1.3

Look at the sentences. In each one, a word is printed in *italics*. These are not English words, but you can understand something of what they mean from the context. Which of the three words a, b or c is the most probable alternative to the words in *italics*?

1. Brian was married with two *kittish* children.
   a sleeping **b** old **c** beautiful
2. Can you give me half a *rote* of cheese, please?
   a type **b** kilo **c** litre
3. This morning, I planted some *zacharoonies* in the garden.
   a flowers **b** fields **c** animals
4. Let's go for a *gack* in the country.
   a walk **b** work **c** talk
5. Mullin opened the book and read the *quinment*.
   a cover **b** book **c** introduction
6. We sat down at a table in the *billcock*.
   a tree **b** lake **c** café
7. We arrived at 5.29 p.m. but the supermarket was already *flupped*.
   a quiet **b** closed **c** expensive
8. Martin was lying on the bed, *granfing* the ceiling.
   a looking at **b** painting **c** talking to
9. I don't mind flying, but I hate waiting at the *grodpost* for hours and hours.
   a station **b** airport **c** aeroplane
10. Sir Geoffrey Cowe, MA (Oxon.), PGDS, DV, is the international *hopplewinger* of the Organisation for Unity in Europe.
    a director **b** politician **c** cleaner

Activity 1.4

In the three passages below, all the words which have been blanked out are different forms of the same word. What is it? Discuss with your teacher.

1. ▇▇▇ is a very popular sport among English people, but it is impossible to ▇▇▇ in England! Some people go ▇▇▇ in Scotland, where there is a lot of snow in winter, but most people travel to France or Switzerland, and spend two weeks ▇▇▇ in the mountains there.

   The word is _____

2. Can you imagine life without ▇▇▇? It's almost impossible to imagine, isn't it? It is strange to give more ▇▇▇ to a plant than many people have to drink.

   The word is _____

3. You can divide homes into two types: with and without ▇▇▇. My mother and father's house was full of them: in the sitting-room, in the kitchen (cookery-▇▇▇, of course), in all the bedrooms (I had 16 shelves of them), even in the toilet. There were boxes of ▇▇▇ in the attic, because there was no room for them in the house. Old, new, thick, thin, ▇▇▇ about love, history, geography, thrillers, novels, guide-▇▇▇, bibles, encyclopaedias, ▇▇▇ with yellow pages, ▇▇▇ with

only one cover, ▓▓▓▓ with no covers, each a perfect jewel, never to be lost or thrown away.

The word is _____

Activity 1.5

Look at the word in *italics*. By looking at the rest of the sentence, can you say what this word probably means? Check your answers with your teacher or a good dictionary.

1. She is a star of films, TV and *the stage*.
2. 'Do you love me, darling?'
   'Yes, darling, I *worship* you.'
3. Tomorrow, my sister and *brother-in-law* are coming to stay.
4. There are no hotels in the village, but there is a *guest house* on the corner of the street.
5. I live in a *hamlet* called Bathbridge; it is about ten miles from the nearest town.
6. John was *fed up*: he had no money, and his girlfriend wasn't speaking to him.
7. She was a very beautiful woman with long, blonde hair and big, *hazel* eyes.
8. Paula walked into the *stable* – the horses were not there!

Activity 1.6

Read about Mary-Jo. Look at the underlined words and guess what they mean from the context. Then complete the definitions, putting the missing words in the crossword.

Hi! My name's Mary-Jo. I'm American. I'm 25, and I'm single, with no children. I live with my brother and <u>sister-in-law</u> (oh, and my little black <u>hamster</u> Tommy) in a large <u>maisonette</u> in Pelham, which is a <u>suburb</u> of New York.

I work as an <u>accountant</u> for Marshall & Tucker. Every morning, I go to work by train. At 11.30 a.m., I stop to have <u>brunch</u> (I don't eat lunch). I get home about 6.30. In the evening I usually go out with my friends – to see a <u>movie</u>, go to a disco or a nightclub. In New York, there's something to do every evening!

Across (→)

2 When she says 'I'm an ACCOUNTANT', she is talking about her _____.
4 SUBURB is probably the name for a part of a _____.
5 SISTER-IN-LAW is probably the _____ of your brother.
6 MOVIE is the American word for _____.

Down (↓)

1 MAISONETTE is probably a kind of _____.
3 HAMSTER is probably an _____.
7 BRUNCH is probably a _____.

Understanding a word from its form

Activity 1.7

An *economist* is a person who studies, or works with, economics.
A *pianist* is a person who plays the piano.

Try and match the words on the left with the definitions on the right. Write the number of the word in the box after the correct definition. The first one is done for you.

1	Biologist	a	a person who works on the front desk of a hotel	
2	Guitarist	b	a person who works with a typewriter	
3	Pacifist	c	a person who does scientific work	
4	Chemist	d	a person who paints pictures	
5	Scientist	e	an expert in the study of animals and/or plants	1
6	Typist	f	a person whose subject is chemistry	
7	Artist	g	a person who plays the guitar	
8	Receptionist	h	a person who believes in peace at all times	

/12/

Activity 1.8

A *dancer* is a person who dances.
A *driver* is a person who drives.

What is the name of a person who teaches?
And a person who writes?
And a person who photographs things?
And someone who cooks things?
And someone who programmes computers?

You probably answered *teacher, writer, photographer, cooker* and *computer programmer*. Now look at these sentences and decide if you were right:

1. My French teacher at school was the nicest man I've ever met.
2. John Needleford, the famous writer, broadcaster and TV personality, has died, aged 66.
3. We've sent a journalist and a photographer to the accident.
4. I've really got to clean the cooker this morning!
5. I'm starting my new job as a computer programmer next week.

You can see that a *teacher* is someone who teaches, but a *cooker* is not someone who cooks, although they both end in –er. You must check the sense from the context.

Look at the words in *italics*. Do they describe a job or not? Look at the context, and put a tick (√) in one of the boxes "Probably", or "Probably not"

	Probably	Probably Not

6. I saw a terrible crash between a taxi and a *tanker*.

7. In England, *dockers* get very good pay.

8. I put the cup on the table next to the *typewriter*.

9. In his 15 years as *night porter* at Clarence's Hotel, Frank Gomes has met many famous personalities.

10. We left the suitcases in a *locker* at the station.

11. My brother works as a *builder*.

12. Is that your cigarette *lighter* on the floor?

13. Jacques Fontana is the best *footballer* in France.

14. a 'What does Helen do?'
    b 'She's a *cleaner* at St Luke's hospital.'

Compound Nouns

Compound nouns are very common in English. Here are some examples:

    tea cup   town plan   course book
    bookshop   chicken soup   bathroom

They are usually in two parts:

    TEA   CUP

So a **tea cup** is a *cup* for drinking *tea*;
a **bookshop** is a *shop* where you buy *books*;
a **bathroom** is a *room* with a *bath*;
chicken soup is *soup* made from *chicken*.

Activity 1.9

Identify and underline the compound nouns in these sentences. (Not all the sentences have compound nouns in them and some have more than one.) The first is done for you.

1. We bought a <u>town plan</u> at the <u>corner shop</u>.
2. I'd like a return ticket to London, please.
3. Do you want to go to the sports centre this evening? There's a good tennis match on.
4. He was wearing a brown coat and a pair of jeans.
5. We decided to meet in the hotel bar.
6. There was a small gas fire in the corner of the room.
7. There's a lovely little fruit market on Wednesdays. It's very cheap and the fruit is really nice.
8. He walked in, sat down, and started reading a magazine.
9. I took the film to a photo shop, but the shop assistant said it was too old to develop.
10. Please do not make copies for personal use with this machine. It is for office use only.

Now look at the compound nouns you have underlined. Discuss with your partner what they mean. Write down your ideas. Talk to other members of the class and your teacher. Do you have the same ideas?

UNIT 2

Predicting (1)

What do you think this unit will be about?

We do not read everything that we see. We do not read every newspaper that comes out every day, or every book that comes into our hands. Often we look at the title and decide if we want to read it or not. We can even say what the book will be about from the title. What do you think these books will be about?

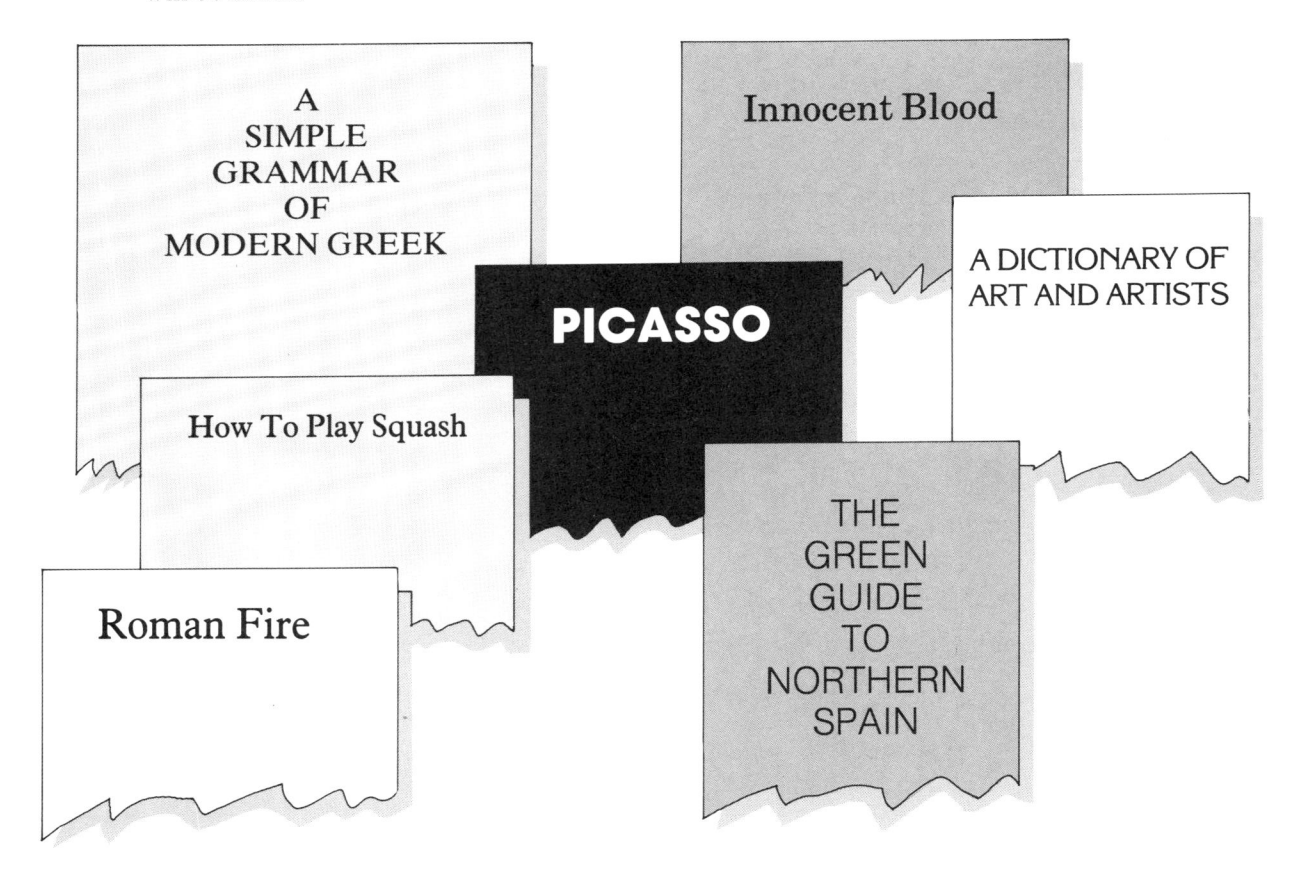

- A SIMPLE GRAMMAR OF MODERN GREEK
- Innocent Blood
- A DICTIONARY OF ART AND ARTISTS
- PICASSO
- How To Play Squash
- Roman Fire
- THE GREEN GUIDE TO NORTHERN SPAIN

Which of these books interest you?

Similarly, when we read a newspaper, for example, we do not often read every part of it. We decide which articles interest us and which articles do not. Some people read only the political articles, others the sport. We can often make predictions about the content of an article from the headline or title.

Activity 2.1
Match the headline with the type of newspaper article. The first one has been done for you.

Headline		Type
1 **MAN KILLED IN TRAIN CRASH**	a	Sports News ☐
2 **GOVERNMENT HUMILIATED IN PARLIAMENT**	b	Medical News ☐
3 2 goals for Rush as Liverpool demolish Arsenal	c	Crime News ☐
4 *The Poet's Voice*	d	Home News [1]
5 **Bush and Gorbachev to meet in Geneva**	e	Political News ☐
6 Computer thief imprisoned for 5 years	f	Arts News ☐
7 CANCER CURE "VERY CLOSE" SAYS LONDON DOCTOR	g	Foreign News ☐

Which of these articles would you like to read?

Activity 2.2
Match the headline on the left with the description on the right.

1 US President in "good condition" after operation | a | An article about tennis. ☐
2 *Spielberg changes direction: not only films for children* | b | An article about a crime in London. ☐
3 **SWEDISH PLAYERS DOMINATE US OPEN SEMI-FINALS** | c | An article about the government's plans to give money to schools to buy computers. ☐
4 2 die in bank robbery in city of London | d | An article about people putting oil into Spanish wine. ☐

5   A COMPUTER IN EVERY SCHOOL BY 1999   e   An article about the cinema. ☐

6   5 MORE PEOPLE ARRESTED IN MADRID WINE SCANDAL   f   An article about the health of the President of the USA. ☐

Which of these articles are interesting to you?

If we can predict what an article or passage will be about, we can understand it more easily. For example, an article in a newspaper has the title 'Life in France 100 years ago'. Which of these subjects will it probably mention?

Computers	The English language
The French language	Pop music
Horses	Fashion
Aeroplanes	Books
Family life	Video-tape recorders

Sometimes, of course, you cannot say what will be in an article. If you could, why would you want to read it? But at other times you can make very close predictions.

Activity 2.3

Imagine you are going to read an article with the title 'Some Rules for Living Longer'. Try and think of six points the article will make.

Now read the actual article which follows. Do you find it easier to understand now that you have thought about what it might say? What do you think the words in *italics* mean?

SOME RULES FOR LIVING LONGER

1 Don't eat too many *fatty* or *greasy* foods, such as butter, the fat on meat, or *fried* foods.
2 Try to take regular exercise – swimming is particularly good.
3 Try and build up a *network* of friends and *acquaintances* – people who have a lot of friends generally live longer.
4 Doctors say that smoking (and drinking to *excess*) is bad for you. If you smoke a lot, try to *reduce*; if you smoke a little, try and *give up*. But small amounts of drink – say a glass of wine a day – can be good for you.
5 *Avoid* stress. (Live in the country rather than the city.)
6 In general, stop *worrying*! People who are *cheerful* and *relaxed* live longer.

It is also very important to try and guess what will come next in a piece of English. We often do this without thinking when we are reading our own language – but sometimes when we read a foreign language, we forget what we do in our own language!

For example, imagine a sentence starts:
George lives in ....

How many ways can you finish this sentence? It could finish with, for example, the name of a country:
George lives in Malaysia.
or the name of a place:
George lives in Frankfurt.
or the type of place:
George lives in a small village.
or the type of house:
George lives in a small bungalow.
or some combination of these:
George lives in a small house in a town near Frankfurt.

Of course, there are lots of possibilities, and you cannot always be exactly correct. But you can give yourself a chance of understanding the meaning in this way. If the sentence in fact finishes:
George lives in a large mansion.
you do not know, perhaps, what a mansion is, but you have thought about the possibilities, and can make a good guess.

Activity 2.4
Finish each of these sentences in three ways:

1   Yesterday I went to visit my _____

2   I really enjoy listening to _____

3   Frank works as a _____

4   I saw a woman reading a _____

5   On the train, there were two men playing _____

You can see immediately that only certain things can come next. For example, sentence 2 cannot finish with *books*, because you cannot listen to a book. You can think about the possibilities – the more information you have, the easier it becomes to predict. If sentence 3 finishes: 'Frank works as a dustman.' you can be sure we are talking about Frank's job; if sentence 5 finishes 'snap', you can say it is probably a game.

Now, use your predictions above: look at these sentences. Can you guess what the words in *italics* mean?

1   Yesterday I went to visit my *nephew*.
2   I really enjoy listening to *R 'n' B*.
3   Frank works as a *blacksmith*.
4   I saw a woman reading a *thriller*.
5   On the train, there were two men playing *draughts*.

Activity 2.5

Cover this passage with a piece of paper. Then move the paper down the page one line at a time. Read each line and every time you see a question try to predict or guess what the answer will be. (There are no 'correct' answers.)

My sister Jane is 32 and works as a
   What does Jane do?
doctor in a big
   A big what?
hospital in London. She likes the job very much but it is very
   Very what?
time-consuming, so she doesn't get much time to
   To do what?
go out in the evenings. Occasionally she goes
   Where does she go?
to the cinema, but if she is not working she usually stays
   Where does she stay?
in and listens to
   Listens to what?
classical music. She isn't married, but she's got a
   Got a what?
boyfriend called Sam, who also works
   Works where?
in the hospital. He's a nurse in the psychiatric wing, so when they're together they usually talk about
   Talk about what?
medicine or medical problems. They are very happy together, but I don't think Jane wants
   What doesn't Jane want?
to get married yet. She is too
   Too what?
busy with her job. Perhaps they'll get married in
   When?
a few years' time.

Activity 2.6

Cover this passage with a piece of paper. Now move the paper down the page, one line at a time. At the end of each line, decide which of the three possibilities **a, b** or **c** is the most likely. Try and decide why you think so.

> Hotel Maribar
> Adipugo
> 14th July 1988
>
> Dear Paul,
> We arrived here on Monday. The flight was absolutely
> **a** good **b** long **c** horrible
> horrible. The plane was late, and there was nothing to eat or
> **a** drink **b** see **c** do
> drink. But the whole journey only took four
> **a** days **b** hours **c** minutes
> hours, and when we got here it was beautifully
> **a** cold **b** foggy **c** hot
> hot and sunny. The hotel is nice: we've got a double
> **a** room **b** bath **c** waiter
> room, with a private bathroom and a large balcony
> **a** who **b** which **c** beautiful
> which overlooks the sea. As for eating, we always have
> **a** breakfast **b** books **c** rest
> breakfast in the hotel, but at lunchtime and in the
> **a** morning **b** evening **c** night
> evening we usually eat out. The restaurants are good, but
> **a** expensive **b** cheap **c** bad
> expensive. Local cuisine is great, but you can eat English
> **a** men **b** beer **c** food
> food if you want.
>   Yesterday in the town we met a very interesting
> **a** woman **b** dog **c** house
> woman called Joy Mackintosh, who, strangely, comes
> **a** and **b** her **c** from
> from Edinburgh, but who now lives in Adipugo. She's a
> **a** painter **b** dentist **c** car mechanic
> painter, and she says she never wants to go back to
> **a** Scotland **b** Adipugo **c** London
> Scotland. Imagine that!
>   Love from
>   Jan

Activity 2.7

Cover the passage with a piece of paper. Move the paper down the page. Every time you see an asterisk (*) decide if the passage continues as in **a** or **b**.

Norman was unhappy. His girlfriend Sally*

    a was nice
    b wasn't talking to him

wasn't talking to him. He didn't know why. When he arrived at school that morning, she was*

    a completely normal
    b at school too

completely normal. But then, at lunch, she came up to his table and said: 'Norman Lewis, you're horrible and disgusting and*

    a I hate you
    b I love you

I hate you!' When he tried to reply, she turned round and walked off. Since then, nothing.
    Norman was unhappy, but he wasn't*

    a very unhappy
    b very happy

very unhappy. That evening, he had a date with Polly Downes from Class 3. Polly was a pretty blonde girl with blue eyes. She spoke with a Welsh accent and was, thought Norman,*

    a very stupid
    b very intelligent

very intelligent (she could speak French). Sally was nice, but she*

    a was prettier than Polly
    b wasn't as pretty as Polly

wasn't as pretty as Polly, and certainly couldn't speak French. Also, Polly was a year older than Sally, who was only seven. This, for a man like Norman (who was eight and a half)*

    a was very important
    b wasn't very important

was very important.

UNIT 3

Using a Monolingual (English–English) Dictionary (1)

A monolingual dictionary is one which uses only one language. So when you look up 'book' in a monolingual dictionary you read a definition in English:

book¹ /bʊk/ *n* 1 a collection of sheets of paper fastened together as a thing to be read, or to be written in

not a translation like *livre, libro, Buch* etc.

Why should you use an English–English dictionary and not a bilingual dictionary with translations into a second language?
 (i) Translations are not always exactly right. Abstract words, especially, are very difficult to translate exactly.
 (ii) Many bilingual dictionaries give a list of translations without clearly explaining the differences between them.
 (iii) Often bilingual dictionaries do not give enough grammatical information.

Which English–English dictionary?

Choose your dictionary carefully. It should:
 (i) be prepared for people who are studying English as a second or foreign language, not for people whose mother-tongue is English
 (ii) use easy words in the definitions
 (iii) be big enough to give clear definitions and example sentences
 (iv) give information about grammar and usage (i.e. when you can use certain words and when you cannot)

For your first dictionary, we recommend:

*Longman Active Study Dictionary of English, Longman, 1983
or *Oxford Student's Dictionary of Current English*, Oxford University Press, 1988

For more advanced work there is:

Longman Dictionary of Contemporary English, Longman, 1988
or *Oxford Advanced Learner's Dictionary of Current English*, Oxford University Press, 1987

* The examples in this unit and also in unit 10 are all taken from this dictionary.

/22/

When do I use a monolingual dictionary?

A dictionary is like a tool:

and not like a crutch:

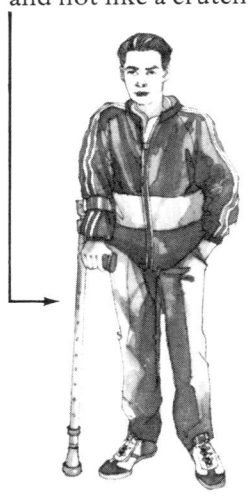

It is very important to read as much as you can without using a dictionary. So remember:

(i) Do not look up the word immediately. Read to the end of the paragraph or page before you decide if the word is important or not.
(ii) Before you look for a word in the dictionary, try to guess the meaning from the form or context (see unit 1).

Can I use a monolingual dictionary to learn new words?

Yes, but not when you are trying to read something. If you concentrate on studying the words you will not follow the text, and if you use the dictionary to understand the text you may not remember the word the next time you want to use it. So don't waste time looking up words you do not need to know!

Alphabetical order

It is important to be able to find words in your dictionary quickly and easily. To do this you need to understand how words are arranged in *alphabetical order*.

Here is the English alphabet – as you can see there are 26 letters:

a b c d e f g h i j k l m n o p q r s t u v w x y z
1 2 3 4 5 6 7 8 9 10 11 12 13 14 15 16 17 18 19 20 21 22 23 24 25 26

Activity 3.1

(i) These words are in alphabetical order. Which numbers in the list above correspond to the first letters of the words? The first one is done for you.

<u>a</u>ll – 1
<u>b</u>all –
<u>c</u>all –
<u>f</u>all –
<u>h</u>all –
<u>t</u>all –
<u>w</u>all –

(ii) These words are also in alphabetical order. The first letter is the same in all the words. Which numbers correspond to the second letters?

s<u>a</u>le – 1
s<u>e</u>ll –
s<u>h</u>ell –
s<u>i</u>ll –
s<u>m</u>ell –
s<u>n</u>ail –
s<u>p</u>ell –
s<u>t</u>ill –

(iii) In these words the first two letters are the same. Which numbers correspond to the third letter?

ca<u>l</u>l – 12
ca<u>m</u>e –
ca<u>n</u> –
ca<u>p</u> –
ca<u>r</u> –
ca<u>s</u>e –
ca<u>t</u> –

(iv) Now, using the alphabet in the same way, write these words in alphabetical order:

a meat _____
   beat _____
   feet _____
   sheet _____
   eat _____
   wheat _____

b top _____
   tell _____
   tall _____
   tree _____
   time _____
   thin _____
   tunnel _____

c those _____
   thug _____
   think _____
   these _____
   that _____
   three _____

d eleven _____
   dark _____
   electricity _____
   deep _____
   eat _____
   elephant _____
   electronics _____
   dinner _____
   electric _____
   dine _____
   eight _____

HEADWORDS AND DEFINITIONS

Look at this sample entry:

> **but‧ter‧scotch** /ˈbʌtəskɒtʃ‖-ərskɑtʃ/ n [U] a sweet food made from sugar and butter (and perhaps sweet SYRUP) boiled together

Here *butterscotch* is the *headword*.

/ˈbʌtəskɒtʃ‖-ərskɑtʃ/ shows the pronunciation of the word in phonetic letters.

n [U] tells us that this word is a noun and that it is uncountable. After each entry in the dictionary there are some letters which tell us about the grammar of the word.

'*a sweet . . . together*' – This is the definition. It tells us the meaning of the word.

Some words have more than one meaning or grammatical category, so you will find more than one headword in the dictionary. Look at this example:

> **lark¹** /lɑːk‖lɑrk/ n infml something done for a joke or amusement: bit of fun: *He only did it for a lark.*
> **lark²** n a small light brown singing bird with long pointed wings, e.g. the SKYLARK

In other cases there is only one headword, but there are several definitions of the word. Look at this example:

> **laun‧dry** /ˈlɔːndri/ n -dries 1 [C] a place or business where clothes, etc., are washed and ironed 2 [U] clothes, sheets, etc., needing washing or that have just been washed

Activity 3.2

Now look at these entries for *second*:

> **sec‧ond¹** /ˈsekənd/ *determiner, adv, n. pron* 1 2nd 2 [C] an imperfect article that is sold at a lower price: *If you want to buy dishes cheaply, you can get factory seconds.* 3 [C] a person who helps another, esp. in a BOXING match or DUEL¹ (1) 4 **second to none** *infml* the best: *As a tennis player Ann is second to none.*
> **second²** n 1 a length of time equal to 1/60 of a minute 2 a measure of an angle to 1/3600 of a degree (or 1/60 of a MINUTE¹ (3))
>
> **second³** v [T] to support (a formal suggestion (MOTION¹ (3)) at a meeting so that argument or voting may follow: *"Will anyone second this motion?" "I second it, Mr Chairman."* -**seconder** n
> **se‧cond⁴** /sɪˈkɒnd‖sɪˈkɑnd/ v [T] BrE fml to move (someone) to a special duty, usu. for a limited time: *Mr Adams was ill, so someone else was seconded to do his work.* -**secondment** n [C; U]

Read these sentences and choose the number of the headword in the dictionary entry which corresponds to the meaning of the sentence. The first one is done for you.

a   Ms Tims proposed that the school should be closed and Mr Johns seconded the motion.
    Headword no. 3
b   The second month of the year is February.
    Headword no. _____
c   There are 60 seconds in a minute.
    Headword no. _____
d   When Mrs Pelham went into hospital, Alison Jones was seconded to do her job during her absence.
    Headword no. _____
e   The perfect plates were very expensive, so I bought some seconds instead.
    Headword no. _____

Activity 3.3

Now look at this entry for *service*:

ser·vice[1] /ˈsɜːvɪs∥ˈsɜr-/ *n* **1** [U] attention to buyers in a shop or to guests in a hotel, restaurant, etc.: *The service in this place is slow/bad. We waited ten minutes for service.* **2** [C usu. pl.] *fml* an act or job done for someone: *You may need the services of a lawyer.* **3** [U] work or duty done for someone: *He died* **in the service** *of his country.* **4** a regular examination of a machine to keep it in good condition: *Take your car for a service/for regular services.* **5** [C; U] a business or organisation doing useful work or supplying a need: *Is there any railway service here on Sundays? a postal service.* **6** [C] a fixed form of public worship; a religious ceremony: *Our church has three services each Sunday.* **7** [C] *esp. BrE* a government department: *the* CIVIL SERVICE. **8** [C; U] (duty in) any of the armed forces: *He saw active service in the last war.* **9** [C] an act or manner of serving (SERVE[1] (7)) in tennis: *He has a good fast service.* **10** [C] the dishes, tools, etc., needed to serve a stated meal: *a silver tea service.* **11** [A; U] (something for the use of) people working in a place, esp. servants in a house: *a service entrance. She was* **in service** *(=worked as a servant) all her life.* **12 at your service** *polite or pomp* willing to do what you command: *If you need any help, I am at your service.* **13 of service** useful; helpful: *(polite) Can I be of service to you?* –compare DISSERVICE

Read these sentences and choose the correct *definition*.

a   You must take the car for a service after the first 5000 kilometres.
    Definition no. 4
b   When the Queen came for tea, they used their best silver tea service.
    Definition no. _____
c   My grandmother is very religious. She always goes to the 11 o'clock service on Sunday mornings.
    Definition no. _____
d   The service in the hotel was so bad that they left after the first night.
    Definition no. _____

e If you want to play tennis at a national level, you must improve your *service*.
   Definition no. _____
f She thanked the accountant for his *services* over the last five years.
   Definition no. _____
g It is not easy to get a job in the Civil *Service* these days.
   Definition no. _____
h There is a regular bus *service* between London and Oxford.
   Definition no. _____
i In many countries military *service* is compulsory for all young men after they finish school.
   Definition no. _____

Activity 3.4

Now use your own dictionary. Look up the words in *italics* in these sentences and write down the number of the headword and the number of the definition:

a He has a *shower* every morning after he gets up.
   Headword no. _____   Definition no. _____
b In Shakespeare's time, the *stage* was in the middle of the theatre.
   Headword no. _____   Definition no. _____
c I bought my father a *record* of classical music for his birthday.
   Headword no. _____   Definition no. _____
d The band played a military *march* as the Queen left Buckingham Palace.
   Headword no. _____   Definition no. _____
e He started swimming when he was very young, but he didn't learn to do the *crawl* until he was 30.
   Headword no. _____   Definition no. _____
f 'Cats' was the last *show* performed in the theatre before it closed.
   Headword no. _____   Definition no. _____

Activity 3.5

Use your dictionary to match the names of the types of food with the pictures. Write the correct names under the pictures:

   chop   courgette   stuffing   haddock   partridge   tangerine   onion
            oyster   cider   pancake

1 _____   2 _____

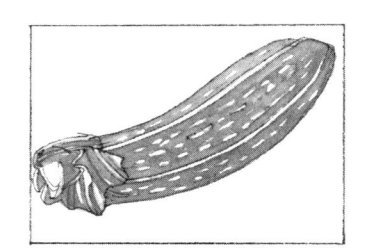

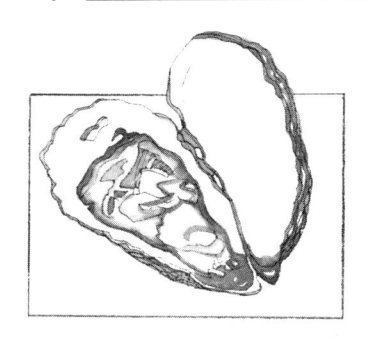

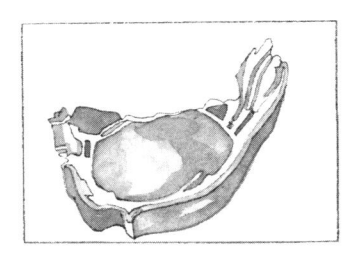

3 _____

4 _____

5 _____

6 _____

7 _____

8 _____

9 _____

10 _____

/29/

UNIT 4

Finding Your Way Around a Text (1)

Many students who need to read English say 'I can understand all the words but not the whole sentence.' One reason for this is that it is sometimes difficult to see how the different parts of a piece of English are connected to each other. For example, a word in one sentence may be talking about something in another sentence.
Here is an example:

   (i) Bill and Mary went to the zoo to see the monkeys.
  (ii) Then they went home for tea.

In sentence (ii), the word *they* is talking about something in sentence (i). What is it? The monkeys? Probably not, because monkeys do not usually drink tea. So it must be *Bill and Mary*. We say that *they* refers to *Bill and Mary*.

This is an easy example, but sometimes in English it is not so clear. This unit will help you with this problem.

Pronouns

Subject	Object	Possessive
I	me	mine
you	you	yours
he	him	his
she	her	hers
it	it	its
we	us	ours
they	them	theirs

Pronouns are used in English in the place of a noun or a name, often to avoid repetition. For example:
   John lived in London. John liked London very much. London is a beautiful city.

In order not to repeat *John* we use *he*, and *it* in place of *London*:
   John lived in London. He liked it very much. It is a beautiful city.

We say that *he* refers to *John*, and *it* refers to *London*. Sometimes it is not easy to see what a pronoun refers to. Another problem is that the pronoun can refer to something which comes after it:
   In his lifetime, Van Gogh was never popular with the public.
     His refers to *Van Gogh*.

Activity 4.1

Draw an arrow from the circled word to show which word the pronoun refers to. The first one is done for you.

1. Ruben says (he) can't come this evening.
2. The Queen was wearing a blue and white dress. (She) was looking calm and relaxed.
3. The shop assistant was tired and upset, but (she) didn't show it.
4. He opened a beer and drank (it) quickly.
5. I don't like cats – (they)'re too independent for me.
6. I wanted to go to the supermarket, but (it)'s closed.
7. The eggs are on the shelves in the kitchen – (they)'re behind the corn flakes.
8. The National Gallery is in Trafalgar Square. (It)'s open every day.
9. The doctor told Hardiman (he) must stay in bed for three days.
10. Lovitt Jeans are for young people, but (they) last until you get old!
11. Put the wine in the fridge – we'll open (it) later.
12. I read in the newspaper yesterday that even before (it) was finished, the Humber Bridge needed repairs.

It is a particular problem, because it has more than one use. Firstly, it refers to objects and things:

This house is beautiful – and (it)'s so big!

But *it* can also be used in certain fixed expressions, especially about the time or the weather:

It's eleven o'clock.
It's raining.
It's all right.

In these cases, *it* does not refer to anything. (You can find another use of *it* in unit 11.)

Activity 4.2

Look at these sentences. They all contain the word *it*. Is *it* part of a fixed expression or does it refer to another word? Tick the box and, if you choose the second box, write down the word *it* refers to. The first two are done for you.

		Fixed Exp.	Refers to …
1	The film was a great success, but I thought *it* was boring.		✓ (refers to … *film*..)
2	Good Lord. *It*'s 5 o'clock already!	✓	(refers to …………)
3	Venice is a wonderful city, but nowadays *it*'s a place for tourists.		(refers to …………)
4	*It* was very foggy on the river, and we were a bit frightened.		(refers to …………)

/31/

5 Peter looked at his watch. *It* said seven o'clock.

☐ ☐ (refers to ....)

6 Joanna looked at the clock. *It* was time to go home.

☐ ☐ (refers to ....)

7 *It* looks much older, but in fact Peebles Hall was only built in 1925.

☐ ☐ (refers to ....)

8 I think American pronunciation is very beautiful, but some people find *it* difficult to understand.

☐ ☐ (refers to ....)

Activity 4.3
Read the following piece and write in the column on the right what the word in *italics* refers to. The first one is done for you.

John got a drum for Christmas. (*It* was a present from Aunt Stephanie.) When *he* opened the box, he laughed and shouted. The drum was John's favourite present; but the family hated *it*. *They* couldn't watch TV or listen to the radio, because John was in the next room, playing *it*; *they* couldn't talk, because *he* was under the table, playing it.
   Finally, father took the drum from John and put *it* away in a safe place. *He* didn't say where.
   John was very upset, but after two days *he* had completely forgotten about *it*.
   'I always thought *she* was mad,' said father.
	the drum
	....
	....
	....
	....
	....
	....
	....
	....
	....
	....

/32/

Words that show sequence of actions or ideas

As in other languages, English uses words which show the organisation of a text:

FIRST   NEXT   THEN   AFTER THAT   FINALLY

These are often used to show the order of a sequence of actions.

Here is an example. While you read the sentences, answer this question: where would you find these instructions?

(i) First, place a plastic cup in the box.

(ii) Then, press the button marked 'tea' or 'coffee'.

(iii) Next, press the button marked 'with' or 'without' for sugar.

(iv) After that, put 10p or 20p in the slot. Tea is 10p. Coffee is 20p.

(v) Finally, open the transparent door and take your cup of delicious tea or coffee.

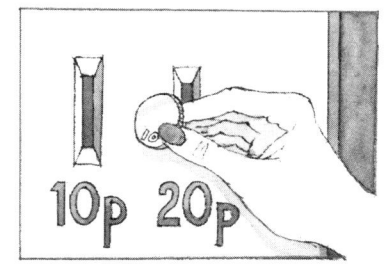

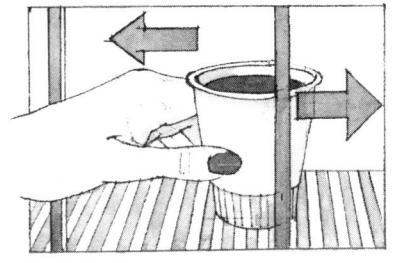

Activity 4.4

Look at the instructions and pictures for preparing spaghetti.

First, put the pictures in order – write a number from 1 to 5 in each of the boxes.

Then decide which instructions correspond to which picture.

Finally, write in the first word of each instruction.

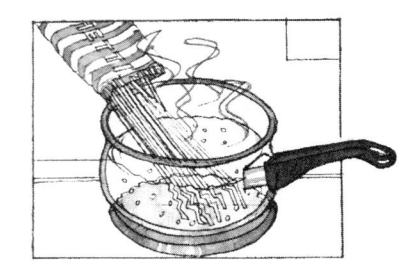

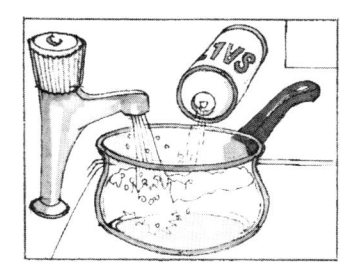

                                Picture

a ...., cook for about ten to twelve minutes. ☐

b ...., add about 80 grams of spaghetti per person. ☐

c ...., drain off the water and serve. ☐

d ...., pour about a litre of water into a saucepan and add salt. ☐

e ...., put the saucepan on the gas and heat until the water boils. ☐

/34/

FIRST/FIRSTLY, SECOND/SECONDLY, FINALLY

These words are often used to indicate a sequence of ideas.

> There are three reasons why I don't like skiing. Firstly, I am not very good at sport; secondly, it's very expensive; and finally, the people who go skiing are horrible!

If you pay attention to these words, you can follow the writer's argument more easily and you will not be distracted by difficult words. For example, let's replace 'it's very expensive' with a more colloquial phrase:

> '... secondly, it costs a packet ...'

You can still understand the *general* sense of the text – you know that 'it costs a packet' is another reason why the writer does not like skiing. There is more work on understanding the general sense of a text in units 5 and 12.

Activity 4.5

Here is an article about British newspapers, which has been cut into pieces and mixed up. Put the sentences in the correct order. Put the numbers from 1 to 9 in the left-hand column, and write the words which helped you to decide the correct order on the right. The first sentence of the article is 6, and it has been done for you. Note that it is not always a single word which helps you to decide.

		Number	Important Words
1	First, they have a lot of news about sport and TV.		
2	These five serious papers have about 1,500,000 readers between them.		
3	There are three reasons for this popularity.		
4	The first type are usually called 'serious' and include *The Times, Financial Times, Guardian, Daily Telegraph* and the *Independent*.		
5	Finally, they often include photographs of good-looking young women.		
6	There are twelve national daily newspapers in Britain.	1	–
7	The second type are often called 'tabloid' newspapers because of their small size, and include the *Sun* and the *Daily Mirror*, which are the most popular papers in Britain.		
8	They can be divided into two types.		
9	Second, they do not have many long or serious articles.		

/35/

Conjunctions

Conjunctions (or linkers) are the words which join together parts of a sentence. You probably already know *and*, *so* and *but*.

> He went home *and* had a bath.
> She's very attractive, *but* I don't like her much.
> Malcolm's feeling ill, *so* we're not going out tonight.

When do you use these conjunctions? Discuss with your teacher.

These conjunctions can help you understand difficult parts of sentences or difficult words. Look at this example:

> (i) She was bored and ......

What does *and* tell us about the missing word?
(a) it is probably an adjective.
(b) it is probably similar to *bored* – a negative adjective.

Can you suggest one?

She was bored and fed up. *Fed up* can mean 'unhappy'.
Here is another example:

> (ii) I was very tired, *so* I decided to ....

What do you decide to do when you are tired? Not much! Any ideas? Maybe you stay at home, go to bed, go to sleep, or even watch TV.

> I was very tired, *so* I decided to turn in. *Turn in* means 'go to bed'.

A final example:

> (iii) She says he's very good-looking, but I don't ....

But tells you that the second half of the sentence disagrees with the first. What words can you suggest to finish the sentence?

Activity 4.6

Match the second part of each sentence (on the right) with the first part (on the left). Use the conjunctions to help you. The first one is done for you.

1	I don't like football	a	and don't touch it again!	
2	There are lots of cinemas in Sidbury	b	so could you please explain it?	
3	I read a lot in the evenings	c	so I didn't go to the match.	1
4	The books were very expensive	d	and do nothing for a month.	
5	The weather was really bad	e	and white.	
6	Put it on the table	f	but there's only one theatre.	
7	Mrs Russell has just bought a cat	g	and I also watch television when there is something good on.	
8	In the summer we go to our house on the lake	h	but we took our umbrellas and enjoyed ourselves anyway.	
9	I don't understand this word	i	so I'm going to borrow them from the library.	
10	Joanna's new shoes are blue	j	and she has decided to call it 'Moggie'.	

Activity 4.7

Here is a simple story in three parts. Each part has been cut into pieces. Put the pieces in the correct order. Use words like *then, so, and, next, first*, and *finally* to help you. Pay attention to the punctuation, too.

PART ONE

a   so I telephoned my friend Julie
b   I didn't want to go by myself,
c   and asked her if she wanted to go too.
d   Yesterday morning I was very bored and fed up.
e   so I decided to go and see a football match.
f   I always feel like this on Saturday morning,

1 _d_   2 ___   3 ___   4 ___   5 ___   6 ___

PART TWO

a   I was ready at last and at 1.15 I left the house.
b   Then I went upstairs
c   We arrived at the football ground at 2.30.
d   and Julie bought a hamburger and chips.
e   and put on my blue and white hat, my blue and white scarf, and my blue and white jumper.
f   Before going in, I bought a newspaper,

1 _b_   2 ___   3 ___   4 ___   5 ___   6 ___

PART THREE

a   First, we bought six cream cakes;
b   and after that to a Chinese restaurant.
c   so we decided to celebrate.
d   Finally, we got home at about 10.30, just in time to watch the match on the telly!
e   next, we went to a pub for a drink,
f   The match finished at twenty to five: our team won 2–0,

1 _f_   2 ___   3 ___   4 ___   5 ___   6 ___

UNIT 5

Skimming and Scanning (1)

We read different things in different ways. Sometimes, we read slowly and carefully because we want to understand something fully, and perhaps remember parts of it. If you look at the list of instructions (on page 46) for travellers to countries where there is a risk of catching cholera, you will understand that it is important to read such an article very carefully!

But think about a telephone directory. Do you read this in the same way? When we want to find a friend's number, we do not start at page 1 and read the whole book until we come to our friend's name. The names are listed in alphabetical order and we look through the book quickly until we find the number we want. In other words, we look for specific information and nothing else. This is called *scanning*.

Now think about reading a newspaper article: often we do not have much time to read a newspaper (on the train, for example, or at breakfast time), so we read the articles quickly, to get the general idea. This is called *skimming*.

Don't forget: scanning for specific information, skimming for the general idea.

Think about these types of English text. How do we read them? In many cases, we do not read everything. Discuss your ideas with other students or with your teacher:

1. the football results
2. a novel
3. a tourist guide
   - a when you are in the street
   - b when you are in bed
4. instructions for building a piece of furniture
5. the review of a new film
6. a price list
7. a menu
8. a telephone bill
9. a business letter

You will see that there are many possible answers – it all depends on why you are reading and what you want to find out.

In this unit, we are going to practise scanning and skimming.

It is very important when you are working on the activities in this unit to remember that you do not need to understand every word.

Scanning

Activity 5.1

Let us start with some practice in scanning. If you are just beginning to learn English, you will probably be interested in information about language schools in England. Imagine you are hoping to attend a course at the Bart School of English this summer. Look at the text and answer these questions about the courses. Work as quickly as possible:

1. How much is a normal course?
2. Why is course C cheaper than the other courses?
3. What kind of sports will you probably take part in at the Bart School?
4. Will you have to pay for textbooks used in class?
5. You want someone to meet you at Heathrow Airport. How much does it cost?
6. You will be 16 on 1st July, and you want to attend course C. Will you be old enough to attend this course?
7. Your friend, Maria, does not know any English. Can she attend the course with you?
8. Which meals will you need to pay for after you arrive?
9. What will you receive at the end of your course?
10. You want to go to London for an excursion on Saturday and Sunday. Is it included in the price?

BART SCHOOL OF ENGLISH

Summer Vacation Courses

Course Dates		Price
A	8th June – 3rd July	£950
B	6th July – 31st July	£950
C	3rd August – 28th August	£930
D	31st August – 25th September	£950

NB There are no lessons on Monday 24th August, which is a holiday in England this year.

Course Fees Include:

23 hours tuition per week
Two sports afternoons per week
Accommodation with an English family,
   with breakfast and evening meal Monday–Friday and
   all meals at weekends
One evening outing per week (disco, party etc.)
Use of textbooks and other material in class
Use of listening centre
Weekly video film
End of course certificate

Course Fees Do Not Include:

extra weekend and evening activities
lunch Monday–Friday

Don't Forget To Bring With You:

a raincoat
a pair of heavy shoes
a towel (sheets are provided)
a swimming costume
a tennis racket

Conditions:

Minimum age limit – 16
Beginners are not accepted. All students must have at least an elementary knowledge of English
All fees must be paid before the beginning of the course
Students may be met at Gatwick/Heathrow airports on payment of a supplement of £40

Activity 5.2

You are now in England. You want to visit some English towns, so you get a British Rail leaflet (you can see the leaflet on the facing page). Answer the following questions about the leaflet as quickly as possible. Do not read everything in the leaflet – just look for the information you need.

1   In or near which town can you see:
   a   23 colleges?
   b   a cathedral dating from 1199?
   c   a castle, 2 parks and a chapel?
   d   the Lanes?
   e   a modern cathedral?
   f   famous flower gardens?
   g   a famous bath?

2   Fill in the following table.
   √ = Yes   X = No   ? = Don't know

	On the sea?	Castle?	Cathedral?	Roman?	Which London station?	Length of journey?
BATH	?	X	X	√	Paddington	1 hour 15 mins.
BRIGHTON						
HASTINGS						
SALISBURY						
YORK						

Day trips from London

Bath
The Roman Spa town of Aquae Sulis. See the Roman Baths, the medieval Abbey and the elegant eighteenth-century architecture of many of the buildings.

⇌ From Paddington at 5 minutes past each hour, on the InterCity 125, British Rail's air-conditioned High Speed Train. Typical journey time 1 hr 15

Brighton
Favourite seaside resort of the Prince Regent (George IV) who built the unique and beautiful Royal Pavilion. Traditional seaside amusements on the beach and Palace Pier, or stroll through the Lanes – winding alleyways full of small shops, many selling antiques.

⇌ From Victoria at 0906, 1005 then at 8 minutes past each hour. Typical journey time 58 min.

Cambridge
A quiet world of learning that hasn't changed much since the Middle Ages. Visit some of the 23 colleges, the oldest dating from 1281, and don't miss King's College Chapel. Stroll along the Backs, the peaceful gardens and lawns bordering the river or better still chance your arm in a punt.

⇌ From Liverpool Street at 35 minutes past each hour. Typical journey time 1 hr 06

Chichester
A lovely country market town between the Sussex downs and the sea, Chichester still retains much of its historical associations. See the 15th century Market Cross, the new Festival Theatre and the magnificent cathedral, dating from 1199.

⇌ From Victoria at 28 minutes past each hour. Typical journey time 1 hr 38

Coventry
The impressive cathedral was completed in 1962, near the ruins of the ancient cathedral. See the breathtaking stained glass, and the huge tapestry.

⇌ From Euston at 10 and 40 minutes past each hour. Typical journey time 1 hr 13

Eastbourne
Fine resort on the South Coast situated beside the high, White Cliffs of Beachy Head. The 3-mile seafront has famous flower gardens, pier and bandstand.

⇌ From Victoria at 53 minutes past each hour. Typical journey time 1 hr 27

Hastings
A delightful blend of old and new on the sunny Sussex coast, this famous old Cinque Port is a town of contrasts. A stone's throw from the bustle of the modern seaside resort, with its 3-mile promenade and 600 ft pier, lies the Old Town, dominated by the ruins of Hastings Castle, originally built by William the Conqueror in 1068.

⇌ From Charing Cross at 45 minutes past each hour. Typical journey time 1 hr 45

Salisbury
An harmonious blend of ancient and modern, Salisbury can justifiably claim to be one of England's most attractive cities. The truly magnificent cathedral with its towering spire, over 400 feet high, is within easy reach of many fine old buildings and the modern shopping centre.

⇌ From Waterloo at 10 minutes past each hour. Typical journey time 1 hr 24

Windsor
Towering over the town and the River Thames is the Royal castle (precincts open daily, Changing of the Guard at 1025). Visit the state apartments, St George's Chapel, the new Madame Tussauds exhibition Royalty and Railways, celebrating Queen Victoria's Diamond Jubilee 1897, or ramble in the Home Park and Windsor Great Park. A 'town trail' guide to the lesser known parts of Windsor is available from the Tourist Information Centre on the station. A short walk away is Eton with its famous school.

⇌ From Paddington (change at Slough) at 35 minutes past the hour for most of the day. Typical journey time 20 mins. From Waterloo at 12 and 42 minutes past each hour. Typical journey time 48 min.

York
Great medieval city of the North with mighty walls, timbered houses and twisting lanes. York Minster, one of England's finest architectural glories, dominates the city which has witnessed events that have shaped the course of English history.

⇌ From King's Cross at 0930, 1100 and 1130. Typical journey time 2 hr 10

Activity 5.3

You are going to find some information from the small advertisements in a newspaper. Read the questions before you read the advertisements.

1. John needs a new bicycle. Write down a phone number where he may be able to get one. _____

2. Peter and Sally have just moved into a new flat and need some new furniture. Write down a phone number for them. _____

3. Philip's washing machine has broken down. Write down a telephone number for him. _____

4. Penny wants to relax in the sun. Write down an address where she can write for information. _____

5. Mrs Fell has bought a computer, but doesn't know how to use it yet. Write down a telephone number for her to phone for help. _____

6. Amanda is holding a party on Friday evening and wants to hire a disco. Write down a telephone number for her to phone to hire one. _____

FIAT 124 1977 Good runner, one year MOT, low mileage. Must be seen! £875. Tel: 848567

HAMMOND Electronic piano & pedal, serviced, excellent condition, £400 o.n.o. 54511

FOR SALE moving to Paris, must sell immediately all furnishings (beds, sofas, tables, wardrobes). From a 3-bedroom flat. Cheap bargains! Ring 9898 or 46700

CAPITAL DISCOS music and light shows for all ages and occasions. 788876

LAWNMOWER wanted. Please tel. 65733

RELAX YOUR mind and enjoy your body at the XERXES CLUB, a holistic health and fitness holiday community on the beautiful Italian island of Elba. Water sports, dance, etc. Details 17 Dobson Avenue, London SE14

MEN'S TOURING bicycle 5-speed 19″ frame 27″ wheel. Rarely used. £80. 76666

DOBERMAN dog for sale. 1 year old, excellent with children, well trained, very good pedigree. 34086

WASHING MACHINES, dishwashers, tumble dryers. Repairs and servicing. 668997

HAIRDRESSING – phone Jan for cut'n blow dry, foil highlights, perming, colouring etc. Your home or mine. Tel. 450167

GIRL'S BICYCLE v.g.c. £45. Record Player with speakers £25. Fridge-freezer £40. 4 stools £1 each. Fish tank on stand £25. 71719

COMPUTER training p/t f/t prog. W.P. Bus. software Amstrad. Zenith's. Tel. 447790

Skimming

Now let us turn to *skimming*. As we said, skimming means looking through a piece of English to get the general idea, or gist. We often read an article quickly, perhaps to see if we want to read it in detail or not, or just to see what it is about.

Activity 5.4

Here are five short paragraphs from newspapers. They are about:

a new book
a volleyball match
a new computer
a picnic
a record

Which is which? Write your answer under the paragraph.

1. The day was beautifully hot, and we decided on a spot just by the river. We took all the food and drink from the hampers and set it down on the grass where Joan
   _____

2. and of course Von Karajan's control of the string section is, as ever, masterly. The orchestra always seems relaxed, and the sounds produced are near perfection. The only doubt
   _____

3. The illustrations are uniformly good, and my children, at least, were laughing out loud when I read them the stories in bed. All the stories are written by well-known authors and it's clear from
   _____

4. think the new arrangements will please users of IBM hardware, but this is not the only reason why Apple have decided to integrate
   _____

5. Chinese team seemed to lose concentration at this point, and their play certainly deteriorated, losing six points in a row. It was only a matter of time before the Russians, whose best player was probably Gor
   _____

We said before that the gist of a piece of English is the general idea. Often it is possible to understand the gist by understanding only a few of the words.

Activity 5.5

You are going to read an article from a magazine for teenagers. Here are ten words from the article. What do you think is the gist of the article?

MODERN   HATE   SCHOOL   PUNK
FASCIST   SCOTLAND   POLITICAL   MUSIC
TEENAGERS   SYNTHESIZERS

Discuss with your partner and teacher. Now read the article. Were you right? (Don't worry if you don't understand every word!)

'WE HATE MODERN MUSIC'
Scots duo in shock claim

'Breaking Eggs' is a new band from Scotland, with a strange mixture of punk and reggae sounds. They're intensely political, and talk about Margaret Thatcher as 'that fascist housewife'. 'Breaking Eggs' is a duo – Pete Sands from Glasgow, and Greg Pollack from Aberdeen.

'We hate synthesizer bands,' says Pete; 'we hate Bruce Springsteen; in fact, we hate nearly everything.' Pete and Greg, both still teenagers, met at school five years ago. 'What we're really into is rebellion.' Their music is hardly modern, but then, as they themselves remark, 'We hate modern music.' Surprise, surprise.

Activity 5.6

Read these three descriptions of jobs. Under them, write the job. Choose from: teacher, taxi driver, doctor, nurse, air hostess, secretary, lorry driver, pilot, bus driver. Don't worry if you don't understand every word.

1
> People think it's a very glamorous and exciting job. OK, so we travel a lot, but we don't see the places we go to. Maybe the girls who fly the American lines manage to visit a place for three or four hours, but when you're on package tours like me, you arrive in one place – Benidorm, say – then immediately you take off back to London.

_____

2
> I love working with children. When they leave the hospital, they're so happy, and it's worth all the hard work. Of course, you sometimes have a real tragedy, like a little girl who came in last week with a rare disease that can't be cured, but that's not very often. And they're so brave! They never cry, even when it really hurts.

_____

3
> I am well-paid, yes, but then I work really bad hours – I'm often away from my wife for days at a time. And it's a difficult job, with a big wagon like this. We've got lots of responsibility. And it's often very boring – hour after hour of motorway.

_____

Which words helped you to decide?

/45/

UNIT 6

Looking for Detailed Information (1)

We said in the last unit that we read different things in different ways. Sometimes we need to find one piece of information from a text; sometimes we need to find the general idea. There are also occasions when we want a full understanding of the passage.

For example, let us imagine that we are going on holiday to a country where there is the risk of catching cholera (which is a very serious illness). We read the list of instructions for travellers there:

> Eat only cooked food – do not eat raw vegetables, and avoid shellfish.
> Drink only bottled water, without ice.
> If there is no bottled water, boil water for a few minutes before using it.
> Never buy food, drinks, sweets or ice-creams from stalls in the streets.
> Keep insects (especially flies) away from food.
> Wash your hands with soap and water before eating and after using the toilet.

In this case, we need to understand (and probably remember) the instructions exactly. And perhaps we feel it is better not to try and guess the difficult vocabulary.

However, these cases are rare. In this unit, we are going to practise extracting all (or most of) the important information from a piece, but without necessarily understanding every word.

Activity 6.1
Read the extract from Susan's letter, and draw the furniture on the plan of the room below.

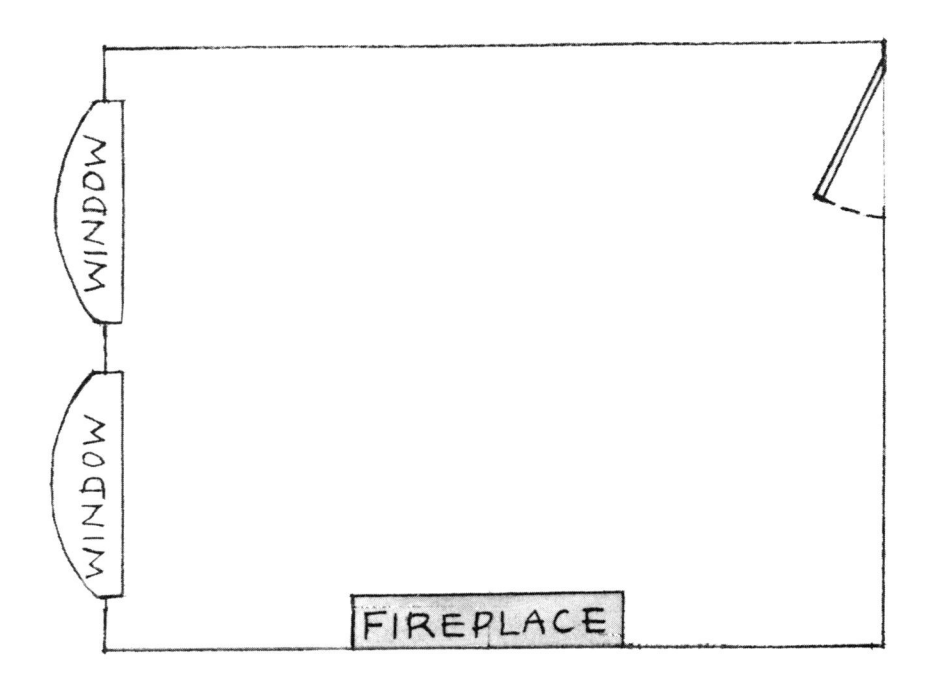

> Dear Mum & Dad,
>   Well – I've arrived! And I've got such a fantastic room. I must describe it to you.
>   I couldn't believe it – it's so big! When you come in the door there's a big fireplace on the left, and on both sides of it there are bookshelves from the ceiling to the floor. Opposite the door there are two large bay windows, and under the one on the left there's a large table with a chair. Along the long wall opposite the fireplace there's a (small) single bed with a very nice sort of Indian bedspread – red and brown. In the middle of the room there are two armchairs – which I've put in front of the fire. But best of all – there's a piano! It doesn't work, but it impresses all my friends. That's just by the door. Oh, and there's a lovely small table where I put my stuff when I come in, just near the door.
>   Now, let me tell you about my first week at the depart

Activity 6.2

Read the newspaper article carefully, and complete the table underneath.

> This week shows little change from last week, with the shopping basket up 4p to 7.65. Best buy among the fruit and veg is courgettes, down from 51p to 49p a pound. Stay clear of mushrooms, which have gone up 10p to 33p a quarter. Apples are up 2p from 44p to 46p a pound, and bananas are unchanged at 52p a pound.
>
> Lamb chops are still a good buy at £1.69 a pound, and beef is down to £2.46 a pound from £2.52. Baked beans can be found at 26p for a large can, down 2p from last week, but corn flakes are up 2p to 85p for a large packet. Finally, bread is unchanged at 59p for a large loaf.
>
> (Information supplied by Marsh Superstores)

	Quantity	Price Last Week	Price This Week
Apples	pound		
Bananas	pound		52
Courgettes	pound		
Mushrooms	¼ pound		33
Lamb Chops	pound		
Beef	pound		
Baked Beans	large can	28	
Corn Flakes	large packet		
Bread	large loaf	59	
Total		£7–61	

Activity 6.3

A Read the letter quickly, then answer these questions:
 1 Who is the letter from?
 2 Who is the letter to?
 3 Is it a business letter or a letter between friends?
 4 What is the main subject of the letter?

> 42 Melbourne Road
> London N2
>
> 23 October 1988
>
> Dear Mike,
>
> Just a quick note to say we've definitely booked our flights, leaving on Sunday 14th December from Gatwick at 14.20 and flying via Pisa to arrive in Bologna at 18.55. Can you meet us? The return flight is on Sunday 21st December leaving Bologna at 15.40 and arriving at Gatwick at 20.40.
>
> Do we need to bring anything - bedding, beds, etc? I hope your flat really is big enough to cope with us all.
>
> There isn't really very much news except to say Brian and Helen popped in last night having just returned from Canada - they don't seem to have picked up much of a Canadian accent.
>
> Well, I haven't got anything else to say. So see you in December. One of us will no doubt write or ring before then.
>
> Love,
> Ken and Jackie

B Now read the letter again and decide whether these statements are true or false:

1 Ken and Jackie are going to visit Mike in December.
2 They are staying two weeks.
3 They want Mike to meet them at the airport.
4 They are going to stay in a hotel.
5 Brian and Helen are probably friends of Mike as well as of Ken and Jackie.
6 Brian and Helen are now in Canada.

Activity 6.4

Read the description of the town and label the map. Some of the buildings have already been labelled.

Coming from Doncaster on the A635, the first building of any importance is the castle, which is on the right. Unfortunately, the castle is surrounded by modern buildings, in particular the Council Offices on the other side of the High Street, and a supermarket next to the castle on the right. The crossroads with Rose Street is the centre of the old town with a pleasant pub, the Cock, on one corner, and the old Town Hall on the other, which is the first of several lovely buildings including the post office and the city museum. Opposite is the public library, an L-shaped building behind a row of trees. On the other side of Rose Street we can find the entrance to the Park, with a small lake to the north, and a new (1984) Sports Centre to the south.

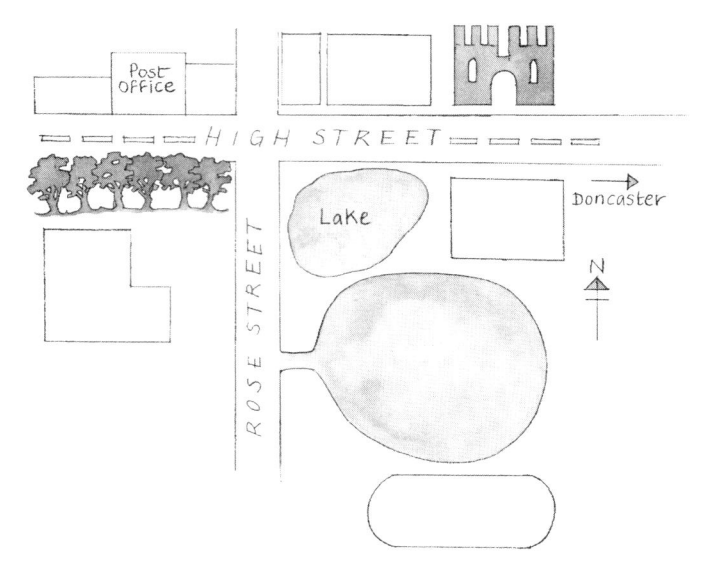

Activity 6.5

Here is a diary for the week. It belongs to a businessman, John Biggs.

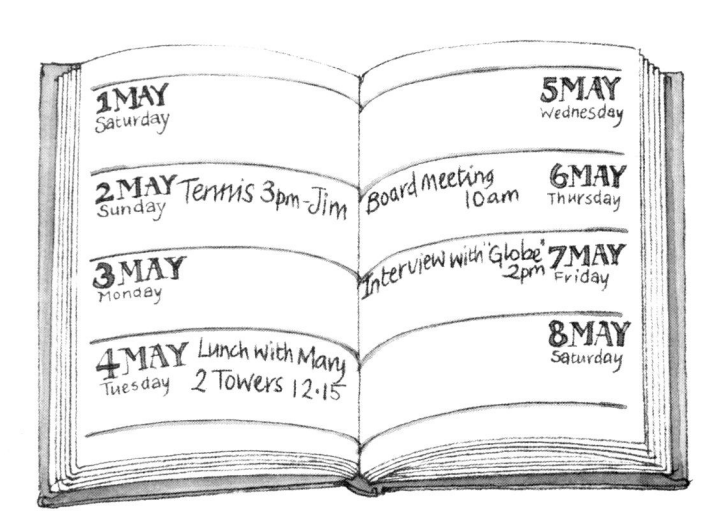

Now read these telephone messages and letters that John Biggs has received and make appropriate changes in the diary.

John Biggs

You are invited to a reception at
CLARIDGE'S HOTEL

Friday 7 May 7.30 p.m.

Black tie
To celebrate 100 years of the
Royal Athenian Society

R.S.V.P.

MEMO

The President's sec. phoned. The board meeting this Thursday has been moved to 11 a.m.

J.C.T.

The Globe

678 Fleet Street, London EC1. Tel: 01-554-1234
ESTABLISHED IN 1876

29.4.8-

Dear Mr Biggs,

Just a note to inform you that I shall be unable to come to your office on 7 May, as we arranged last week. I have been posted to Iran on an important assignment, and I shall be out of the country for several weeks. Many apologies for this.

Yours sincerely,

Paul Morris

J.B.

I'm going to Paris for the weekend. We'll have to change the tennis. Let's play the Saturday after — the 8th. Same time - Ok?

Jim

John,
Can't make Tuesday for lunch. What about Wednesday?
Sorry!
Mary

John Darling,
I must see you! How about ~~supper~~ on Wednesday evening at Maxim's - 8 o'clock.
See you there.
Love
Lucy.

Activity 6.6

Read the text below and complete the family tree. Some of it has already been done for you. If you can't find the information, put a question-mark (?).

Hello! My name's Jill Bennett, and I live in Dublin. I work as a bus driver for the local bus company. I'm 32, and I'm the eldest of four. My brothers and sister are called Stella (she's the youngest), Luke, and Frank. Strangely, they're all married except me. Stella's husband is called Brian, and they haven't got any children. Stella married very young: she's only 22 now.

Luke's next – he's 24, and he's just started working as a junior doctor in a hospital in London. His wife's name is Ruth, and she's a doctor too. They've already got a little baby, Douglas, who was born last year. Finally, there's Frank, who's 31, and who's married to Dorothy. They've got two children, Ken, who's six and Millie, who's four.

We all live in different parts. I was born in Manchester in the north-west of England, and that's where my Mum still lives. She lives in a small council house just outside Manchester; she lives on her own – our Dad died in 1982. Stella lives quite close, in Bolton, but Frank lives in the USA. He's got a fantastic job with an American company called Pleximusk, and they transferred him to New York.

```
                    ┌─────┐ ┌─────┐
                    │ DAD │=│ MUM │
                    └─────┘ └─────┘
                    Died ......   Lives in
                                  ....................
```

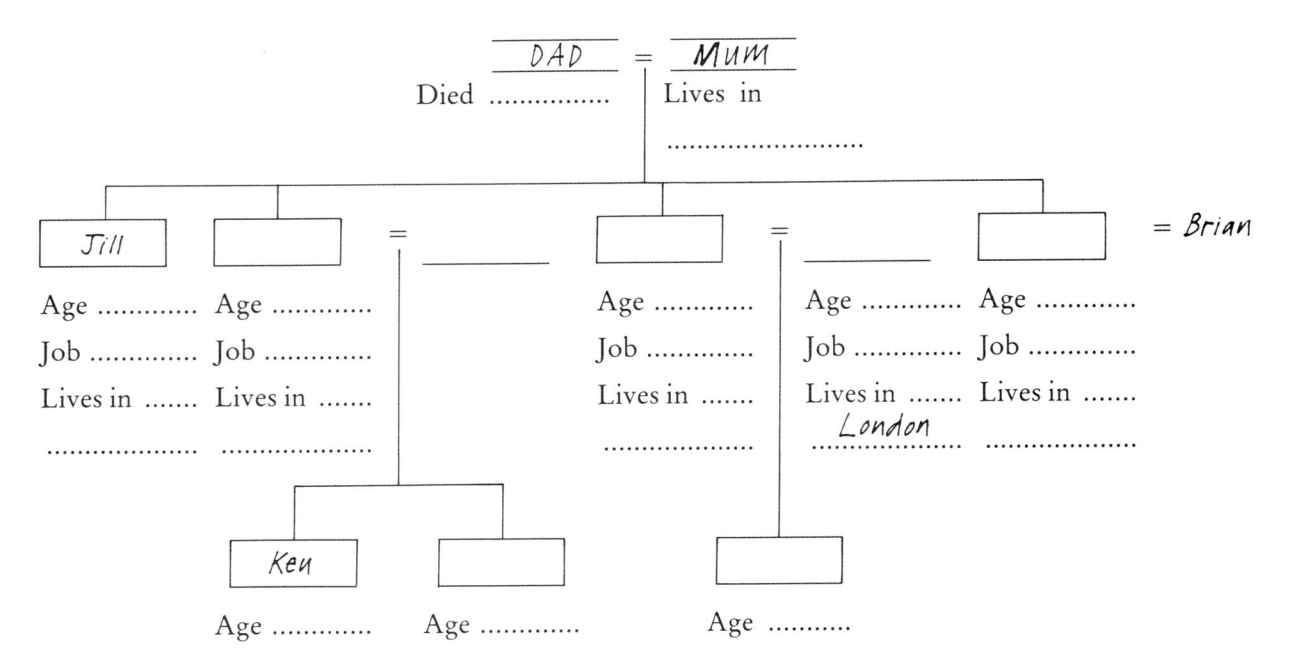

```
┌──────┐  ┌──────┐         ┌──────┐         ┌──────┐  ┌──────┐
│ Jill │  │      │ = ...   │      │ = ...   │      │  │      │ = Brian
└──────┘  └──────┘         └──────┘         └──────┘  └──────┘
```

Age ....   Age ....   Age ....   Age ....   Age ....
Job ....   Job ....   Job ....   Job ....   Job ....
Lives in .... Lives in ....   Lives in ....   Lives in .... Lives in ....
....   London   ....

```
         ┌──────┐  ┌──────┐         ┌──────┐
         │ Ken  │  │      │         │      │
         └──────┘  └──────┘         └──────┘
```
         Age ....   Age ....   Age ....

Activity 6.7

Imagine you have arrived in an English city, and see an information poster about the buses in the city. Complete the tables on p. 54 with information from the poster.

BTB BUS COMPANY

The BTB Bus Company serves all parts of the city, and also provides an extensive service to nearby towns and villages.

BTB CITY BUSES are usually **orange**, and operate from 06.30 to 23.30. There are four kinds of ticket you can use:

TOURIST RANGER is the ideal ticket for tourists and visitors to the city. The tickets are valid for 2, 3, or 5 days, and can be used on all city buses. They cost £4, £5.50 and £7.50.

MONTHLY SEASON – Going to work by bus? This is the one for you! For only £26.50 you have the freedom of the city for a whole calendar month.

BUS CARD – lasts for one day. For £2.50 you can travel anywhere on the bus system for one day – but you must clip your card in the machine every time you board a bus.

SINGLE JOURNEY – 50p. Valid for just one journey. Clip the ticket when you get on the bus. Books of ten tickets also available.

These tickets are only valid on BTB City Buses. They are available from post offices, tobacconists and BTB offices. TICKETS CANNOT BE PURCHASED ON THE BUSES.

BTB COUNTRY BUSES (which are usually **blue**) serve the towns of Conby, Rashville and Grill as well as numerous villages in the area. Services run from 07.00 to 21.30.

TICKETS are bought on the bus. The minimum fare is 75p, increasing with distance. Buses depart from the main railway station and Goshley Square.

A MAP of the routes for both City and Country buses can be obtained (price 20p) from the BTB offices at the main railway station or 27 Park Square. Timetables for both services can be found at the bus stops.

Table 1

BTB City Bus Tickets		
Name of ticket	How long does it last?	How much does it cost?

Table 2

	City Buses	Country Buses
Colour of buses?		
Where do they operate?		
Where do I buy tickets?		
Minimum fare?		
What time of day do services operate?		
Where can I find timetables?		

UNIT 7

Mixed Skills (I)

So far, we have practised reading in different ways – predicting what comes next, guessing difficult words, skimming, scanning, etc. – but when we read in real life we often do all these things at the same time. This unit will help you to use these skills together by providing you with several activities to do on the same piece of English.

Activity 7.1

A Scanning
Read this letter quickly and answer the following questions:
1. Who wrote the letter?
2. Is the letter about a car, a washing machine, or a cassette recorder?

> 15 Marsh Road,
> Wallsend.
> 8th March 19--
>
> Dear Sirs,
>   On 4th March, I bought a Hypersonic cassette recorder, price £47.50, from the Wallsend branch of your company. On 5th March, at precisely 6.32 p.m., it broke down.
>   I took it back to the shop, and talked to an assistant, Mr Delaney. Unfortunately, he was very rude, so I asked to speak to the manager, who told me that, as I did not have a receipt, the shop could not give me a new recorder.
>   I must say that I am very disappointed with the service in your shop, and I would be grateful if you would send me a refund immediately.
>   Yours faithfully,
>   Anne Jones (Mrs)

B Skimming
What does Mrs Jones want?

C Guessing Difficult Words
Find the words below in the letter. Use the context to decide if they mean **a** or **b**. Do not use a dictionary.
1. *branch*: **a** shop **b** house
2. *precisely*: **a** nearly **b** exactly
3. *broke down*: **a** stopped working **b** started working
4. *rude*: **a** beautiful **b** not polite
5. *as*: **a** when **b** because
6. *receipt*: **a** a letter from the shop
             b a piece of paper saying you have paid
7. *disappointed*: **a** unhappy **b** ill
8. *refund*: **a** cassette recorder **b** money back

D Looking for Detailed Information

Read the letter again carefully, and decide if the following statements are true or false. Put T or F in the box after the statements, as in number 1.

1   Mrs Jones lives in Wallsend. ☐T☐
2   She wrote the letter four days after she bought the cassette recorder. ☐
3   She bought the recorder in Wallsend. ☐
4   The recorder broke down after only 48 hours. ☐
5   The manager of the shop was very rude to Mrs Jones. ☐
6   The shop did not give Mrs Jones a new recorder because they did not have one. ☐
7   Mrs Jones would like to buy another cassette recorder from this shop. ☐

Activity 7.2

A Read the letter from European Education, and tick which of the following instructions are contained in it, possibly in different words:

1   Please come for an interview. ☐
2   Please do not come for an interview. ☐
3   Write a reply to this letter immediately. ☐
4   Telephone our office to fix a time. ☐
5   Follow these directions to get to our offices. ☐
6   Please send us some money. ☐

European Education

CEILING HOUSE, JACKSON'S GREEN, KENT CT14 3PD
Tel: 0232–75414   Cables Euroed   Telex 644893

TD/PDC

Miss J. Johnson,
14 Garth Close,
King's Lynn,
Norfolk.   12th September 19--

Dear Miss Johnson,

Thank you for your recent application for a position as a resident representative with European Education for the forthcoming winter season.

I am pleased to inform you that you have been selected to attend an interview which will be held at these offices during the weeks beginning 24 September and 1st October 19--.

Would you please telephone this office on receipt of this letter to arrange a mutually convenient time for your interview.

If you are travelling by train, Ceiling House is ten minutes' walk from Jackson's Green Railway Station. Turn left out of the station and at the first pedestrian crossing, turn into Bromyard Road until you reach the Methodist Church. Follow the road round to the right and Ceiling House is immediately on your left-hand side. European Education offices are on the first floor. If you are attending by car, there is a large, free car park behind our offices.

Travelling expenses only to the value of the return rail fare from London Bridge to Jackson's Green will be paid.

Yours sincerely,

Terry Donaldson
Terry Donaldson
Continental Manager

B Now read the letter again and answer these questions:

1 The interviews will take place from _____ _____ to _____

2 You must telephone this number: _____ _____

3 Which is the office, A, B, C, or D?

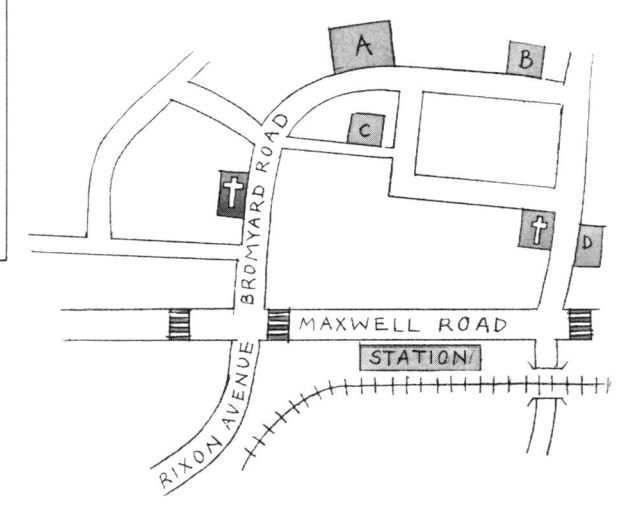

Activity 7.3

In this activity, you have to complete various exercises, using the same text.

A Predicting

Read the title and look at the picture. What do you think the passage will be about? Discuss with your partner and your teacher.

B Skimming

Read the passage and put the pictures which follow in the order in which they occur in the story (not the order in which the writer mentions them). Write the number of each picture in its box.

A STRANGE EXPERIENCE

It was 11.30 at night, and we had just come back from the pub. I was staying in a youth hostel in Ireland with some friends. It was in an old castle about 20 miles from the nearest town. We were the only guests that night. The warden of the hostel was an old man of about 75 who had a funny eye and false teeth.

We went to bed immediately – we were exhausted after a long day's walking. But at about 3 in the morning I woke up and heard the most extraordinary sound – I heard a choir singing! At first I thought it must be a record player, but then I realised it was coming from the trees outside my window. I got up, opened the window, and the sound got louder. I couldn't believe it, so I went over to my friend Frank's bed, and woke him up. He could hear the choir too, so I wasn't just imagining it.

In the morning, I asked the old man if he had heard the singing during the night. He looked angry and a bit puzzled. 'There's no choir here! They're dead long ago!' he shouted. But he refused to say any more, and I never found out what it had been.

C Pronouns

What do these pronouns in the story refer to?

1 it (line 3)   =   *the youth hostel*
2 we (line 4)   =
3 it (line 12)   =
4 him (line 16) =
5 he (line 20)   =
6 they (line 22) =
7 it (line 24)   =

/58/

D Compound Nouns

Look at these compound nouns in the text. What do you think they mean?

1 youth hostel (line 2)
2 false teeth (line 7)
3 record player (line 12)

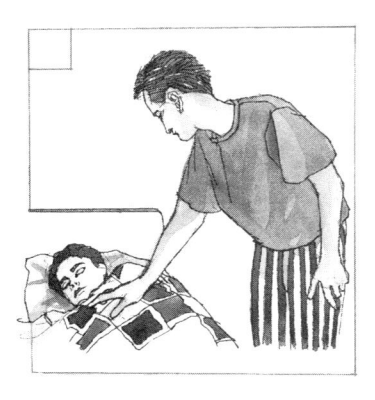

E Guessing difficult words
Choose the best definition for these words from the text:

1 warden (line 5)
   a person who looks after a hostel
   b guest in a hostel
2 funny (line 7)
   a strange
   b entertaining
3 exhausted (line 8)
   a very happy
   b very tired
4 choir (line 11)
   a group of singers
   b bird
5 shouted (line 22)
   a spoke loudly
   b spoke softly
6 found out (line 23)
   a told
   b discovered

Activity 7.4

In this activity, you have to carry out various activities on the text.

A Skimming and Scanning

Read the piece about Portmeirion quickly (maximum one minute) and answer these questions:

1 Portmeirion is   a a town in England
                    b a village in Wales
                    c a village in Italy
2 Who designed Portmeirion?
3 When is Portmeirion open to the public?

PORTMEIRION

Portmeirion is one of the strangest places in Britain. It's an Italian village – on the coast of Wales!

Where is it? Portmeirion is situated on a beautiful peninsula near Caernarfon in North Wales.

What is it? Portmeirion is the creation of Sir Clough Williams-Ellis, Wales's most celebrated architect, who designed and built the strange and attractive village over a period of 50 years. He bought the peninsula (then called Aber Iâ) in 1925. The village is full of villas and mansions, domes and spires, lawns and ponds, brightly coloured houses and cottages.

Surrounding the village on all sides are the wild gardens. These contain an extensive collection of rare plants and flowers from Japan, the Himalayas and Australia.

Can I visit it? Yes. Portmeirion is open to the public from 9.30 a.m. to 5.30 p.m. every day from 1 April to 31 October. The entrance fee is £1.70p.

Is it possible to stay in Portmeirion? Yes. You can stay in one of the cottages in the village or, from 1988 onwards, in the Hotel Portmeirion. A double or twin room with private bathroom is £16 low season and £18 high season (per person sharing). Breakfast is additional. It is also possible to stay in the 20 self-catering cottages sleeping from 2 to 8 people.

Portmeirion Shops As you stroll through the village, you will notice several shops. You can buy books, gifts, jewellery, ladies' and children's fashions and antiques; or, as a souvenir of your visit, why not take home some elegant Portmeirion pottery?

B Guessing Difficult Words. Find these words in the text. Which of the three definitions a, b, or c, is the best? (Do not use a dictionary!)

1 *peninsula:*

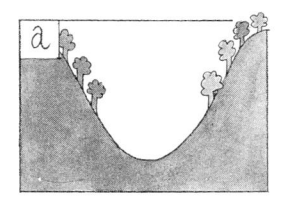

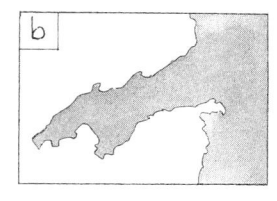

2 *celebrated:* **a** rich **b** tall **c** famous
3 *surrounding the village on all sides:*

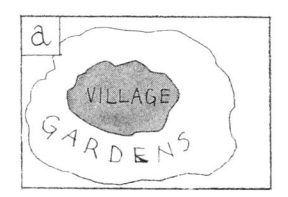

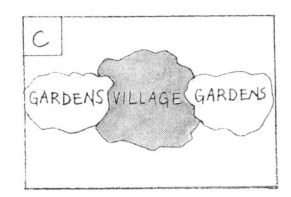

4 *from 1988 onwards:* **a** until 1988 **b** during 1988
   c during and after 1988
5 *twin room:* **a** room with one big bed
   b room with one big bed and two small beds
   c room with two small beds
6 *additional:* **a** very good **b** included in the price
   c not included in the price
7 *stroll:* **a** run **b** drive **c** walk slowly
8 *pottery:*

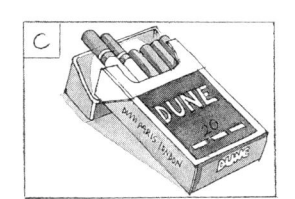

C Detailed Understanding. Answer these questions, using information from the article:

1 Where is Portmeirion?
2 When did Sir Clough Williams-Ellis buy the peninsula?
3 What can you find in the gardens?
4 Is Portmeirion open to the public in the winter?
5 How much does it cost to get in?
6 What do you think *self-catering* means?
7 Are there any shops in the village?
8 What can you buy there?

Section B

UNIT 8

Guessing Difficult Words (2)

Even if you are very good at English – in fact, even if you speak English as your first language – you will often meet new words when you are reading; but, as we said in unit one, there are a number of good reasons why you should not use a dictionary:

  (i) stopping every five seconds to look up a word can interrupt your reading;
 (ii) your dictionary may be too small or too old;
(iii) you may not have a dictionary with you;
(iv) many people believe that if you learn a word without looking it up in the dictionary, you remember it more easily.

So how can we understand these new, difficult words? We have two possibilities:

a we can try to understand the word from the context;
b we can try to understand the word from its form.

Understanding a word from its context

What do we mean by the *context*? We mean the words and sentences around the difficult word. It is very useful to be able to guess (or estimate) the meaning of a word from its context. You may not understand it exactly, but you can probably understand it enough to go on reading.

Sometimes, the context is very clear; if we have a picture, for example, understanding is easy:

LION

At other times it can be more difficult. Here is an example:

Activity 8.1

Look at sentence one (in the left-hand column) and follow the instructions (or answer the questions) in the right-hand column. Do not read sentence two until you have followed all the instructions for number one. Then do the same for two, and continue with all the sentences (there are five altogether).

1	YESTERDAY I SAW A WOPPERGLOT.	Think about the word *wopperglot*. What can it mean? Your first reaction is probably 'anything', but this is not true. Can it mean 'water'? Can it mean 'love'? Can it mean 'a radio programme'?
2	IT WAS IN THE STREET OUTSIDE MY HOUSE.	Any more ideas? What can you see in the street? Which of your ideas about the first sentence are now not possible?
3	IT WAS BIG AND WHITE.	Which of these are now possible? a a kind of animal? b a kind of tree? c a man? d a bus or lorry?
4	I THINK IT WAS GERMAN...	What can you see in the street which is big, white and German?
5	...BECAUSE IT HAD A SIGN WITH 'D' ON THE BACK.	What do you think now?

Now try some other activities to help you guess the meaning of words from their context.

Activity 8.2

Read this note on the next page from a mother to an au-pair girl. Do the underlined words correspond to picture a, b or c? Why?

Patricia

1. Please heat some soup in a saucepan for the children's dinner.

2. Could you change the sheets on Philip's bed?

3. I want to make a cake. Can you please buy some icing-sugar?

4. Please water the cactus in the sitting-room.

5. Shirts and socks are in the green bucket in the bathroom — please wash them.

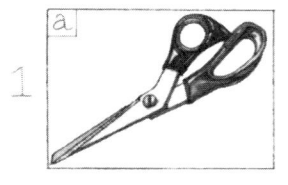

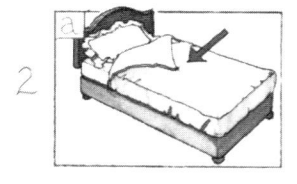

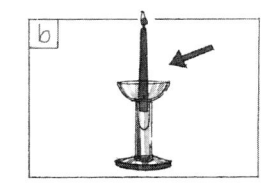

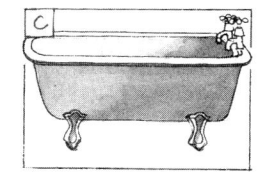

Activity 8.3

All the words which have been blanked out in the following passages are the same word (sometimes in a different form). Look at the context, decide what the word is, and write it underneath the passage. Then write the words that helped you to decide.

1   When we went inside, the ▓▓▓▓▓ had already started, and there was complete darkness. We looked for a seat, but I remember the first scene of the ▓▓▓▓▓ took place at night, so there wasn't any light from the screen to show us where to sit. Finally, a woman with a torch came and helped us. It was only at the end of the ▓▓▓▓▓ (which was terrible, by the way) and the lights came on, that we realised we were the only people there.

The word is _____

The words which helped you decide are _____

_____

2   People nowadays often complain about 'convenience foods' – you know, food that comes in tins or packets – but in many ways the ▓▓▓▓▓ is the perfect convenience food. It has its own container – though we call it a shell. You can keep it in the fridge for some time. It can be used for all kinds of different dishes – omelettes, cakes, pancakes – or you can have it fried, scrambled, boiled or poached. Of course, ▓▓▓▓▓ are full of cholesterol and probably very bad for you. But who cares?

The word is _____

The words which helped you decide are _____

_____

3   I studied ▓▓▓▓▓ at University, but I didn't like it. The problem was that I was interested in buildings of all kinds – churches, castles, houses, factories – but not at all interested in becoming an ▓▓▓▓▓ myself. The ▓▓▓▓▓ courses at University taught you to design new buildings (with some reference to the ▓▓▓▓▓ of the past, of course). But I hate modern ▓▓▓▓▓ – I prefer to sit for an hour looking at a mediaeval church or Gothic cathedral.

The word is _____

The words which helped you decide are _____

_____

Activity 8.4

Read the following sentences and look at the words in *italics*. Then answer these questions:

a What part of speech are they (i.e. verb, adjective, noun, adverb, participle, preposition etc.)?
b What ideas have you got about what they mean?

1. I went to the shops and bought some apples and *ghorks*.
2. Yesterday we went *zilching* in the mountains.
3. Michael's dog had long, *trubby* hair.
4. We left the bucket *fraus* the kitchen door and waited.
5. Since 1945, British society has *declementated* very much.
6. He read the passage *inkfully*.
7. Eric's wife was a *labber* before they got married, and now she works as Eric's secretary.
8. I stayed in a lovely *borilla* in Corfu for two weeks.
9. He *prealed* himself if he really liked Sally.
10. Deborah had eaten five or six cucumber sandwiches and was feeling a bit *inaldate*.

Now discuss your ideas with your partner and your teacher.

Activity 8.5

Look at this conversation. Where there is a space, look at the context and think of a word which can go in the space. Then write the word in the crossword, according to the number. The first is done for you.

Paul: Morning, Mr Rogers.
Mr R: Good morning, Paul. Please sit down. How is your wife?
Paul: Not very well, I'm afraid. Last night she couldn't ___8→___.
Mr R: Oh, dear, I'm very ___11→___.
Paul: Yesterday, she went to the ___1→___, and he gave her some medicine...
Mr R: Yes, I see. Now, Paul: what time did you arrive in the ___4↓___ this morning?
Paul: Um... well... 10 o'clock.
Mr R: Yes, Paul, 10 o'clock. And ___6↓___ it was 11.30.
Paul: But, Mr Rogers, my wife is in bed, so I have to make ___9→___ for myself, so I always arrive late.
Mr R: 11.30?
Paul: Er, well, yes... er... yesterday I arrived at the station, but there was some problem with the ___5→___.
Mr R: What sort of problem?
Paul: Er... it was very ___7→___.
Mr R: And why didn't you catch the earlier one?
Paul: Well, I went to the station restaurant to have a cup of ___2↓___. And when I was drinking it, the train came in. So I caught the next one instead. Then after five minutes, the train stopped. And it ___10→___ there without moving for half an hour. Then finally, when I got into the Underground, there were lots of people waiting to buy a ___5↓___ ...

Mr R: OK, Paul, enough. But tomorrow, make sure you get here on time.
Paul: Ah, well, actually, Mr Rogers, I'd like a day's holiday tomorrow. My wife's ____3→____ is coming for the day, and I'm cooking lunch...
Mr R: No, Paul, no. No, no, no, no, no, no ....

Activity 8.6

Look at the words in *italics*. Decide from the context what you think they mean, and prepare to demonstrate by miming. No dictionaries!

1. I was walking down the street when I *slipped* on a banana skin.
2. At the end of the concert, the audience *clapped* enthusiastically.
3. Every time I put pepper on my food, I start *sneezing*.
4. I didn't see the cat asleep on the floor, and I *tripped* over it.
5. When I got to the barrier, the security man *frisked* me very carefully.
6. He *struck* a match and lit his cigarette.
7. He *shook* his head and said, 'No, thank you'.
8. The old woman *patted* the boy on his head and gave him £5.
9. Johnson opened the suitcase, put the gun inside, and *shut* it again.
10. 'What's Jim doing?'
    'He's *sweeping* the kitchen floor.'
11. He *undid* his buttons and took his shirt off.
12. The medicine was horrible: he *swallowed* it quickly.

Understanding a word from its form

Let us imagine that we have decided a word is important for our understanding of the passage we are reading. Unfortunately, the context does not give us enough information about the meaning. What can we do?

One possibility is to examine the form of the word. Many words in English are connected with each other by form – and so, also, by meaning:

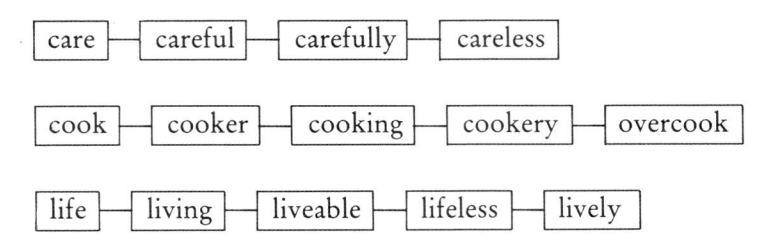

care — careful — carefully — careless

cook — cooker — cooking — cookery — overcook

life — living — liveable — lifeless — lively

For example, we said in unit 1 that words which end in –er often describe jobs: *teacher, driver, writer*. But if they are adjectives, they may be the comparative form: with short adjectives like *hot, small,* or *long*, we add –er to the adjective if we want to compare two things:

Oman is a *hotter* country than England.

or we can add –est to the adjective if we want to compare three or more things:

The Amazon is the *longest* river in South America.

This can be difficult for students reading English. You must decide from the sense if a word is a comparative or superlative adjective or not.

Activity 8.7

Look at the words in *italics* in these sentences. Are they comparative or superlative adjectives or not? If they are, tick (√) the sentence and write the original adjective.

1. The *earliest* train leaves at six.
2. We went along the *forest* road, and arrived at the house.
3. This town is *smaller* than it was ten years ago.
4. Last year she married a *bomber* pilot called Warren.
5. This is probably the *greatest* film ever made.
6. Miss Universe is the name of a beauty *contest*.
7. The man I was meeting was sitting at a table drinking a cocktail: he was *fatter* than I expected; too fat for a secret agent, I thought.
8. Mary's cat was the *fastest* thing on four legs in the whole town.

Word formation

When you are starting to learn English, there are some words which you learn very soon; for example, simple adjectives:

warm   long   strong   young   happy   rich
cold   famous   tired   old   poor   beautiful

or common nouns:

friend   bread and butter   business   man   hair
toilet   office   sun   fire   orange

We can use these words to help us guess the meaning of new words that we meet. For example, if we see the word *happiness*, we can guess that it is connected with the word *happy*. Then we can use the context to check if we are right:

Before I met Sally, I didn't know what happiness was.

Activity 8.8

All the words in the following list are connected with one of the words in the lists above. Write the word in the space. The first one is done for you.

tiredness _____ *tired* _____   beauty _____   strength _____

friendly _____   toiletries _____   poverty _____

official _____   warmth _____   fiery _____

sunny _____   buttery _____   fame _____

oldish _____   hairy _____   orangeade _____

Activity 8.9

Each word in the right-hand column is connected with a word in the left-hand column. Can you match them? (They all begin with P to make it more difficult!) The first is done for you.

1	permit	a	pronunciation	☐
2	please	b	purify	☐
3	proud	c	preparatory	☐
4	pig	d	permission	1
5	pure	e	pride	☐
6	person	f	pleasure	☐
7	play	g	piggish	☐
8	pronounce	h	personnel	☐
9	prepare	i	playful	☐

The situation is sometimes complicated by *affixes* (bits of words like dis– or pre– or –less).

Activity 8.10

Here are some words which are probably unfamiliar to you. Can you think of a more familiar word with which they are connected? Write them in. The first one is done for you.

heartening ____*heart*____   helpful _____

knowledge _____   youth _____

heat _____   boredom _____

hunger _____   enrich _____

endanger _____   explanation _____

But, as we said before, you must be careful, because sometimes you can think a word is connected with another word when in fact it isn't. Look at this:

'How's Johnny today, Mrs Roberts?'
'Oh, I'm afraid to say he's a bit poorly today.'

You might think that *poorly* is connected with the word *poor* (meaning 'without much money') but if you look at the context you can see this is not possible. What do you think *poorly* means from this context?

So you must still check the meaning from the context.

Activity 8.11

Look at the words in *italics* in the following sentences. Each word is similar to, or connected with, a very common English word. Write down the common word in the space provided, and write a very simple definition, using the context to help you. The first one is done for you.

1 Arthur is a very *talkative* man – sometimes he speaks for twenty minutes without stopping!

   Common word: ____*talk*____

   Definition: ____*likes talking*____

2 I like my coffee *milky*.

   Common word: _____

   Definition: _____

3 It was a very *rainy* day, so we decided to stay at home.

   Common word: _____

   Definition: _____

4 I don't recommend a *cycling* holiday in the Alps.

   Common word: _____

   Definition: _____

5 Is your new house *furnished*?

   Common word: _____

   Definition: _____

UNIT 9

Predicting (2)

We have already said that it is important to try and look ahead in a text and guess what will happen next. In our own language we do this without thinking.

When you read any kind of book, magazine or newspaper, there is nearly always information outside the text which tells you something about it: for example, on the cover of a book there is a blurb, which describes the content of the book and tries to persuade you to buy it. There are titles, headlines, sub-titles, photographs, pictures. You should try and use these as much as possible – if you know something about what you are going to read you will find it much easier.

Activity 9.1

Look at these titles of newspaper articles. What do you think the article will be about? Choose **a** or **b**:

1 Presidential visit to China

a The President is going to visit China
b The Chinese President is visiting this country

2 THE SEARCH FOR A CURE

a The story of an operation
b An article about research into cancer

3 The Rise of a Superstar

a How a film actor became famous
b An article about astronomy

4 LA to TOKYO IN 2 HOURS

a A visit from some people from Los Angeles to Tokyo
b A new plane

5 *The Voice of an Angel*

a An article about religious faith
b An article about a singer

6 GIVING TVs BRAINS OF THEIR OWN

a New TVs with computers in them
b Making TV programmes which are more intelligent

7 The Comeback of the Camel

a Camels are being used successfully again
b A story about a camel's return home

8 Life with the Lions

a The story of a family who lived in Manchester
b The biography of a woman who lived in Africa

9 CIGARETTE WARS

a A war between two countries about tobacco
b The battle between tobacco companies to sell more cigarettes

Activity 9.2

Here are the titles and introductions to some articles from newspapers and magazines. Read the texts and think about the content of the articles. Put √ if you would like to read the article and X if you would not. Then turn to page 74 and look at the activity.

1 ☐ **TRAIN AND FIRE ENGINE IN DEATH CRASH**

Second accident in a week on level crossing

2 ☐ **HOME AT LAST!**

Brave little Tim says goodbye to the nurses after twelve weeks

3 ☐ **WAITER!**

Among the young people of London, eating out is now a very fashionable pastime – right up there with dressing well or driving the right car. Jon Sargent reports.

4 ☐ **STORIES FROM THE OUTBACK**

Opening in London this week is a new Australian film, *Snakes and Ladders*, an epic story of life and love down under. But the author of the original book, Judy Nelson, has had a more incredible life than any film. Fran Thomas met her in Sydney.

5 ☐ **SPEAKING FRANCKLY**

French film-maker Franck Yvart has been working in Hollywood for ten years. His latest film *Dreams* has caused controversy on both sides of the Atlantic. KATIA LORD found the director very willing to talk about it...

6 ☐ **SUMMIT TALKS**

Earlier this year, a joint US–USSR party of mountaineers tried to climb Annapurna, one of the world's most fearsome peaks. But politics was the least of their problems. Report by Don Smith, who accompanied the party.

7 ☐ SLOGGING IN THE SUN

Are you reading this on the beach at Brighton, or in a hotel in Hastings? If so, have you ever thought of spending your summer *working* in a holiday resort? You won't earn much money, but you'll have lots of fun! Lisa Leigh met some seasonal sloggers down on the coast.

Activity 9.3

Look at these questions. In which of the articles in 9.2 do you think the reporter asked these questions? Write the number of the article in the box after each question. There are two answers to some of them.

a   When did you first start writing? ☐
b   What are the main problems with this particular mountain? ☐
c   What made you come to Brighton for the summer? ☐
d   How old is he now? ☐
e   How often do you eat out each week? ☐
f   When did the accident happen? ☐
g   How long did your boy have to stay in hospital? ☐
h   Do you prefer using English or your own language in your work? ☐
i   Do you ever eat fish and chips yourself? ☐
j   How fast was the train going? ☐
k   How long did it take you to write the book? ☐
l   What's the most fashionable restaurant in London? ☐

Activity 9.4

You are going to read a short article with the title:

A DAY IN THE LIFE OF A TENNIS STAR

Fulvia Krashinova, born in Russia, but now an Australian citizen, describes her typical day.

Before you read the article, write down seven things that you expect Fulvia to talk about. Number 1 is done:

1   *getting up*
2   _____
3   _____
4   _____
5   _____
6   _____
7   _____

Now read the article and tick (√) the items you predicted correctly.

"MY DAY begins at 6.30. My coach

Doug Braines wakes me up. I go jogging down on the beach here at Teemaine for 20 minutes, or maybe half an hour. Then I have breakfast – usually eggs, bacon, toast, orange juice, coffee, yoghurt. I love breakfast – it's my favourite meal of the day. Then at 8 or 8.15 I'm out on the courts here, practising with Doug. We practise for an hour or two. Every day we concentrate on one aspect of my game – my serve, say. That's the part I like best – just playing tennis!

From 10 to lunchtime, I don't do anything special, maybe go swimming in the pool here, or in the sea. I try not to have a big lunch, but sometimes I have to meet with my sponsors – that's Obibat, the sportswear people – so maybe we have a light lunch in a restaurant.

In the afternoon, I go to the gym for a couple of hours, doing weight-training, building up my body. Lots of women players don't worry too much about their physical condition, but I think it's really important. I'm very fit, and I plan to stay that way!

After that comes study. If we've got a big championship like Wimbledon coming up, we spend a couple of hours thinking and talking about it – we look at videos of my main opponents, discuss strategy, etc. Then another hour on the court with Doug, putting it all into practice.

In the evening, I like to get out and forget about tennis. There's a lot of life in Teemaine, so I try to get to a disco or club. But I don't go to bed too late – 11.30, 12 at the latest. I'm a good girl!"

Predicting is also important when we read a piece of English, not only before. Sometimes you can understand a sentence more easily if you know what kind of word is coming next. The best way to learn this is to read as much as possible in English and familiarise yourself (even without thinking!) with English sentence structure. But you can also do exercises to help yourself. Look at this:

Mrs Jones always ...

What kind of word will come immediately after 'always'?
An adjective?

Mrs Jones always *interesting* ...

No!
A noun?

Mrs Jones always *table* ...

No!
A verb?

Mrs Jones always *goes* ...

OK! Let's go on:

Mrs Jones always *goes* to the ...

Preposition? No. Verb? No. Noun? Could be:

Mrs Jones always goes to the *market* on Fridays to buy some ...

Verb? No. Noun? Could be: ... to buy some *bread*.
Adjective? Could be: ... to buy some *fresh* fish.

Activity 9.5

Read these sentences and try to say what the next word is going to be: verb, noun, preposition, etc. Sometimes two or three different answers are possible. Discuss with your partner and teacher.

1 At that moment, I could not ...
2 There was nothing to see from the ...
3 When she came back, five ...
4 'I'm not going to ...
5 At a quarter to six, I said goodbye to Mary and George and walked ...
6 She was dark and ...
7 The weather was very beautiful that autumn when we first began ...
8 Would you like an ...?

Of course, English is a very flexible language, and there are always a large number of possibilities for the next word. Often it is more useful to try and predict not the next word, but the next few words or the next phrase.

Activity 9.6

Finish these phrases or sentences in any way that seems appropriate to you. Then discuss with your teacher.

1 The robber is described as being in his late 20s, 1 metre 74 cm tall, with black hair, and wearing ...
2 In bed, I lay listening to ...
3 When Alison Cuthbertson moved from London to the outskirts of Nottingham, she couldn't find a job ...
4 As soon as she left the hospital, she went into town and bought herself ...
5 A 65-year-old teacher and his wife were recovering today after spending most of New Year's Day ...
6 My grandfather strongly believed that the last World War made everybody ...
7 Just before the start of the tour, he bought a new house on a hill in a ...
8 Child psychologists have described the presence of animals in the home as ...

Activity 9.7

Cover the text with a piece of paper. Move the paper down the page one line at a time. When you see an asterisk (*), try to guess the next word or words. There is more than one correct answer.

Once upon a time, there was a
princess who lived in a very big *
_____ near the sea. She was very *
_____, but unfortunately she wasn't very *
_____, because her father, who was
the King, didn't want her to meet other *
_____. He wanted her to stay in and *
_____.

One day, she heard the sound of *
_____ in the garden outside her window.
She looked out and saw an old woman playing a *
_____. The old woman said to her:
'Are you happy, my dear?' The princess *
_____, 'No, I'm not. I haven't got any
friends. Can you help me?'
At this point, the old woman
took out a little green frog from her *
_____ and gave it to the princess.
'If you kiss this frog, it will become
anything you want.' Then the old woman *
_____. The princess kissed the frog,
but it remained exactly the same.
The princess was very *
_____. 'What a pity!' she said to
the frog. 'I hoped you would become a *
_____.
'Oh, yeah?' he replied. 'And what's wrong
with frogs?'
Moral: some frogs are very * _____.

Activity 9.8

Cover the passage with a piece of paper. Move the paper down the page one line at a time. Stop when you come to a question. Try to answer it in any way you think appropriate before you continue reading.

Albert Freeman was celebrating
   What was Albert celebrating?
his 64th birthday at his Devon home when he
   What happened?
received the best present he's ever had –
   What was it?
an £85,000 win on the football pools. 'I'm not thinking about
   About what?
what I'll do with the money until
   Until when?
I've recovered from the shock,' he said. Mr Freeman has done the pools for
   For how long?
years, but the win is his first success. 'It's marvellous news,' said
   Said who?
his wife. 'This is a super birthday present. We still can't
   Can't what?
believe it.'

Activity 9.9

Cover the text on the following page with a piece of paper. Move the paper down the page one section at a time. After each section choose from the three alternatives on the right (a, b, or c) how you think the piece continues.

Some people like shopping for clothes; others enjoy buying furniture, or food, or fish and chips. But I like buying books. When I go into a big bookshop, I feel

    a sick.
    b very excited.
    c rather unhappy.

very excited. I often go to Glasgow on Saturdays to get some food for the weekend, but I usually spend the whole day (or, at least,

    a the whole morning)
    b a lot of the evening)
    c I think so)

the whole morning) in one of the city's book stores. Partly it's the smell of new books which attracts me, partly the colour and variety of the covers; or maybe it's the knowledge of the pleasure

    a you can have in bookshops.
    b when you come out of the shop.
    c that reading can bring.

that reading can bring.
   But, although new books are nice enough, it's second-hand books which

    a cost the most.
    b I really hate.
    c I really love.

I really love. For me, a book consists of the words in it – not the glossy cover or the elegant printing. If I can find for 20p a book that costs £4 new, I consider it

    a a wonderful bargain.
    b money I can use for something else.
    c very bad news indeed.

a wonderful bargain. Which is why I view the gradual disappearance of second-hand bookshops with great sadness. So many of my happiest days have been spent in them, often buying nothing, but always

    a buying something.
    b looking at books.
    c enjoying myself.

enjoying myself. New books are interesting, but second-hand books are

    a interesting too.
    b a wonderful and secret world.
    c cheaper.

a wonderful and secret world.

UNIT 10

Using a Monolingual (English–English) Dictionary (2)

It is important to understand something about English grammar so you can use your dictionary easily.

Nouns and Verbs

In English many words can be both nouns and verbs. You can usually decide from the context if a word is a noun or a verb. Look at these examples:
 (i) They went to the theatre to see a *play*.
(ii) The children *play* in the garden after school.
In (i), *play* is a noun. In (ii), *play* is a verb.

Activity 10.1

Look at these sentences. If the underlined word is a noun, write *n*; if it is a verb, write *v*. Like this:

1 She gave him an angry look.   *n*
2 Look at this photograph.   *v*
3 He enjoys his work very much.
4 We work in the centre of London.
5 I cook for my family every day.
6 My brother is a cook in a restaurant.
7 This is a plan of the house.
8 We plan to go to Jamaica this summer.
9 I always fly to London because it's faster than going by train.
10 Look! There's a fly in my soup.
11 He bought a new sail for his boat.
12 They sail among the Greek islands every summer.

Now check your answers in the dictionary. You will see that there are different headwords or definitions for the nouns and verbs. Sometimes the meaning is similar; at other times the meaning is completely different. So when you look for a word in the dictionary, decide first if it is a noun or a verb (or neither). You will save time.

/79/

Verbs

When you look for a verb in the dictionary, you will usually find the base form: *look, play, wait*. When you are reading, you will often find the verb in different forms:
looking   played   waits – in these cases it is easy.
The headwords are   *look   play   wait*

Verbs with regular past tenses and past participles end in **–ed**, but other verbs have irregular past tenses and past participles.

When you look up *fell* in the dictionary you will find:

fell¹ /fel/ *v past tense of* FALL¹

So you must look under *fall* to find the definition of the word.

fall¹ /fɔːl/ *v* **fell** /fel/, **fallen** /ˈfɔːlən/, **falling** [I] **1** to descend through the air: *He fell off the ladder.* |*The stone fell 10 metres before reaching the bottom of the well.* **2** to come down from a standing position, esp. suddenly: *She slipped and fell (down/over).*| *Five trees fell over in the storm.* **3** to become lower in level, etc.

Here you can see the three parts of the verb and the definition.

Activity 10.2

Read this passage and underline the past tenses. How many regular and how many irregular past tenses are there? (Notice that *fed* is an irregular past tense.)

> When school broke up in June, the children rushed back to the country where they knew lots of fun awaited them. They spent most of the summer out in the fields where they learnt about farm life. The labourers fed and milked the cows and goats, fed the chickens and collected the eggs, harvested the wheat and ploughed the fields, picked the fruit and sent it off to the town for sale. The children helped whenever possible but sometimes they created more problems than they solved.

Write the base forms of the verbs in the passage:

Regular verbs   **Irregular verbs**

_____ _____   _____ _____
_____ _____   _____ _____
_____ _____   _____ _____
_____ _____   _____ _____
_____ _____   _____ _____

/80/

Now use your dictionary to help you understand the passage.

Activity 10.3

Use your dictionary to complete the table:

Base form	Past tense	Past participle
fall	fell	fallen
	swam	
		woken
	understood	
		known
become		
	cut	
	flew	
		worn
	won	
		sold
	wrote	

Now prepare another exercise like this for a friend.

Idioms and phrasal verbs

Sometimes it is difficult to understand a phrase even when we understand all the words in the phrase. This is often because the words, read together, have a different meaning from the individual words.

Idioms

Activity 10.4

There are a lot of idiomatic expressions in English. They are listed in the dictionary under the most important (key) word. The key word is usually a noun, a verb, an adjective or an adverb. Try to choose the key words in the idioms in *italics* in these sentences:

1. She was really *over the moon* when she passed the exam.
2. Eva and Tony are *going through a bad patch*. I hope they don't decide to divorce.

3 You really *pay through the nose* in that restaurant.
4 I'll stay with you *through thick and thin*.
5 For the first five years of their marriage, Eva was *under Tony's thumb*.
6 When the police *got wind of* his arrival in Exeter, they started looking for him urgently.

Now look up the idioms in your dictionary. Can you find them? If not, choose another key word and try again.

Now discuss in groups, or with your teacher, what these sentences mean.

Sometimes a word can have many different meanings, especially when we find it in idiomatic expressions.

Activity 10.5

Look at the entry for *get* in your dictionary.
Now look at these sentences with *get* in them. Using your dictionary, match the meanings of *get* with the definitions below. The first one is done for you.

1	Lots of animals get killed every year.	*be(are)*
2	I got a letter from my brother today.	
3	Don't worry. I'll get the supper today.	
4	The food is getting cold.	
5	We got there at 6 o'clock.	
6	How are you getting to Paris?	
7	Don't go out in the rain. You might get a cold.	
8	I don't get it. Why did he do that?	
9	I can't get channel 2 on my TV set.	
10	Can you get me some milk from the shop?	

```
understand    travel       be      catch     receive
become    find/hear/see    arrive    cook      buy
```

Phrasal verbs

In English many verbs are followed by prepositions or adverbs and often the meaning of the verb changes with each different preposition or adverb. For example:

GET has many meanings
   Mary is very popular. She *gets* a lot of letters. (receives)
   Your dinner is *getting* cold. (becoming) etc.
But *GET UP* has a different meaning:
   I always get up at 7.30. (leave the bed)
And *GET OUT* has another meaning:
   Get out of my house! (leave)

We must learn to look for the meanings of these phrasal verbs as quickly as possible. Look at the entry for *come* in your dictionary. The first entry – *come* – is followed by *come* + preposition or adverb in alphabetical order. So we see:

come about *v adv* [I + *that*] to happen: *How did this dangerous state of affairs come about?*

come across¹/upon sbdy. /sthg. *v prep* [T *no pass.*] to meet or discover, esp. by chance: *I've just come across an old friend I haven't seen for years.*

come across² *v adv* [I] *infml* to be effective and well received: *Your speech came across very well: everyone liked it.*

come along *v adv* [I] **1** also **come on–** to advance; improve, esp. in health: *How's your work coming along?|Mother's coming along nicely, thank you.* **2** to happen; arrive by chance: *I got the job because I came along at the right time.*

Activity 10.6

Now match the words in *italics* in these sentences with the explanations below, using your dictionary to help you. The first one is done for you.

1 The police have decided to *come down* heavily *on* people who sell drugs. ____*punish*____

2 *Look out!* The road is icy! _____

3 I can't *make out* what you're saying. _____

4 He decided to *give up* smoking. _____

5 The thieves *got away* with all the money. _____

6 I want to *find out* where he lives. _____

7 Eva and Tony have *fallen out*. _____

8 Mary couldn't *put up with* the noise any longer. _____

9 She *passed away* after a long and happy life. _____

10 What's *going on* here? There's a lot of noise. _____

understand	argue/quarrel	be careful	die
escape	punish	happen	stop
	discover	tolerate	

/83/

UNIT 11

Finding Your Way Around a Text (2)

Have you ever stopped reading a piece of English and said to yourself: 'How strange! I don't understand this! The words aren't difficult, but I still don't understand the sense.'?

As we said in unit 4, we often read something which seems easy but which we do not understand very well. In this unit, we are going to help you with some common problems of this kind.

A No Pronoun

Example: The man Philip saw was Greek.
Problem: There is a noun – *man* – followed immediately by a name – *Philip*. Is Philip the man? And a verb *was* after another verb *saw*. How is this possible?

This sentence is really two sentences put together. The two sentences are:
  (i) Philip saw a man.
  (ii) The man was Greek.

It is possible to put a relative pronoun like *who, which* or *that* in the sentence:

The man who Philip saw was Greek.

but in these kinds of sentences (and especially in spoken English) it is often not included. Here is another example:

The book I am reading at the moment is really interesting.

This is like saying:
  (i) I am reading a book at the moment.
  (ii) This book is really interesting.

When we try to understand sentences like this, we first decide what the main sentence is. So:

The ship Captain Cook sailed in was called *Discovery*.

The main sentence is:
The ship was called *Discovery*.

We can now ask the question: 'Which ship?' Answer:
The ship Captain Cook sailed in.

Activity 11.1

Look at these sentences and see if you can complete the gaps. The first one is done for you.

1. The book I was reading had a blue cover.
   Main sentence: *The book had a blue cover*
   Which *book*? *The book I was reading*

2. The new car we've just bought has broken down already.
   Main sentence: _____
   Which _____? _____

3. The story I would like to tell you is called 'Cinderella'.
   Main sentence: _____
   Which _____? _____

4. The chair he was sitting on suddenly collapsed.
   Main sentence: _____
   Which _____? _____

5. Let's go to that film John was in.
   Main sentence: _____
   Which _____? _____

6. The glasses you gave us have been very useful.
   Main sentence: _____
   Which _____? _____

7. The part of the city I was talking about was near the castle.
   Main sentence: _____
   Which _____? _____

8. I saw the man you work with the other day.
   Main sentence: _____
   Which _____? _____

9. The insect Robinson discovered lives in Brazil and Ecuador.
   Main sentence: _____
   Which _____? _____

10. The novels Dickens wrote at the end of his life were very sophisticated.
    Main sentence: _____
    Which _____? _____

B This/That

Example: Too many people nowadays are only interested in money. In my opinion, this is a cause of many of the world's problems.
Problem: What is the cause of many of the world's problems? Money?

The words *this* and *that* are used by writers to guide the reader to something in a different part of the text:

> Klou painted *Rubbish* in 1965. This was his most controversial work so far.

The problem can be: what does *this* or *that* refer to?
They can refer to a single noun, a phrase, an idea, or a complete paragraph:

> Tony said he was leaving me. This made me very unhappy.

Sometimes, in fact, you do not know what *this* or *that* refers to! Most of the time, we can work it out from the sense.

Activity 11.2

What does *this* or *that* refer to in these extracts? Choose from a, b, or c. (Sometimes it is not clear.) The first one has been done for you.

1 Many young people take drugs and drink alcohol. This makes me very sad.
   a alcohol
   (b) young people taking drugs and drinking alcohol
   c young people

2 Two letters arrived, including the postcard from my aunt. I read this quickly, but it said nothing.
   a the postcard
   b the two letters
   c it is not clear

3 Senator Wilma Marsh has written a document called *Nuclear Power: The Choices*, saying nuclear power is too dangerous. I do not think the President understands this, however.
   a the document
   b that Senator Marsh has written a document
   c that nuclear power is dangerous

4 Pamela only sent me one letter all year and that made me really angry.
   a the letter
   b the fact that Pamela sent only one letter
   c it is not clear

5 Watching TV is the most popular activity among 5–10-year-old children, research done at the University of Rochester has found. Most parents knew this already.
   a the research
   b that some research has been done
   c that watching TV is popular among young children

6 I wanted to put the sofa in the corner opposite the TV, but Jill didn't like that.
   a the TV
   b it isn't clear
   c the idea of putting the sofa in the corner

7 Jack and Phyl came for tea the other day. (You know they're engaged now, don't you?) That was nice.
   a the fact that Jack and Phyl are engaged
   b the tea
   c the fact that Jack and Phyl came for tea

8 First, I telephoned you. Then I sent you the photograph of you and me. This was returned. Finally, I sent you a telegram.
   a the telephone call
   b the photograph
   c the telegram

9 We went to a pub near my house, and after that he took me to a lovely little Malaysian restaurant. But this was the best part – we went to Buttermint's Night Club!
   a it isn't clear
   b going to the restaurant
   c going to the night club

C Elegant Variation

Example: Sally's new cat was sitting in the garden. Cuddles was a magnificent animal.
Problem: Are the two sentences talking about the same thing, or about different things? Is Cuddles a cat?

Writers often refer to the same thing in different ways, perhaps to avoid repetition, or for poetic or literary effect:

> Jack could see all of Paris from his window. The city twinkled and sparkled in the sunset.

Here *the city* obviously refers to Paris – but at other times the connection is not so clear:

> Filbertson hated flying so much that just looking at a plane made him nervous. As he waited in the airport lounge for his call, he thought about the monster outside, ready to eat him up.

Does this mean that there was a monster outside on the runway? No, of course not. *Monster* is another way, perhaps a more vivid way, of describing the plane.

Activity 11.3

Look at these passages. Find two or more different references (not pronouns) to the same thing. Put a circle around the words or phrases. The first one has been done for you.

1. Sue Raymond's (first novel) was published in 1982. (The book) was a phenomenal success.
2. Nancy sat in the café, drinking coffee and waiting for her husband. Where was the stupid man?
3. We arrived back at the hotel at midday. Even in hot sunshine, the building seemed somehow evil.
4. Strathgorn is a village in the north-east of Scotland. It is a silent, tranquil place. But now the small community is to be transformed.
5. Ethiopia, Mali and now Mozambique – three countries in Africa with terrible food and water problems. What can the rest of the world do to help the continent?
6. Roland Begel, who was elected President of the USA in November, moved into the White House today. The leader of the world's most powerful nation said he was happy and proud to be the head of a great country, and said he would do everything to ensure peace and prosperity for the 'Queen of Democracies'.

D Conjunctions

Example: The sun shone brightly in the African sky. Despite this, we decided to go out.
Problem: Did they decide to go out <u>because</u> it's hot?

If we understand the meaning of conjunctions (which are the words which join sentences and phrases), we are in a much better position to understand the whole of the sentence. In unit 4, we looked at the conjunctions *and, so* and *but*. Here are some more:

1	2	3
also as well (as) in addition (to) furthermore what's more	although even though though however despite in spite of whereas yet	therefore consequently as a result

The conjunctions in group 1 are used to join similar ideas, and so are similar in meaning to *and*. Group 2 has words which join opposite or disagreeing ideas, and so are like *but*. Group 3 has words which express the idea of something happening because of something else, and are like *so*.

Here are some examples:

(i) He's strong and fit. He's { also very intelligent. / very intelligent as well.

The house is too small for us. In addition, { it's too far from Mum's.
    Furthermore,
    What's more,

(ii) Even though { the film was very long, we enjoyed it.
    Although
    Though

I liked the film very much. However, I don't want to see it again.

Despite { being very tired, we decided to have a game of tennis.
In spite of

Italy is a republic, whereas Britain is a monarchy.
You say you don't like fish, yet you eat it every day!

(iii) Last year we did not manage to sell as many cars as we wanted.
    As a result,
    Consequently, } we have decided to close down the factory in Liverpool.
    Therefore,

Activity 11.4

Cover the exercise with a piece of paper. Now move the paper down the page one sentence at a time. The first sentence you will see has a space. Look at the rest of the sentence, especially the conjunction, and write a possible word or words in the space. (There is no one correct answer.) Then look at the second sentence, which has the space filled with a difficult word. Do you think the word in the space means the same as your word or words?

Continue the exercise in this way, and then check your answers with a dictionary.

1 a Although it was _____, we went out for a walk.
    b Although it was pouring down, we went out for a walk.

2 a In the sports centre, there are two tennis courts, as well as a _____ and a basketball court.
    b In the sports centre, there are two tennis courts, as well as a football pitch and a basketball court.

3 a We did not give the plant enough water. As a result it _____.
    b We did not give the plant enough water. As a result it perished.

4 a He's very lazy. In the evening he just watches TV, and, what's more, he *never* helps me with the _____.
    b He's very lazy. In the evening he just watches TV, and, what's more, he *never* helps me with the chores.

5 a My brother is good with his hands, whereas I'm more _____.
    b My brother is good with his hands, whereas I'm more intellectual.

6 a AIDS is a terrible disease which has no cure. Yet the government has given only limited _____ for medical research into AIDS.
b AIDS is a terrible disease which has no cure. Yet the government has given only limited funds for medical research into AIDS.

7 a There has been no rain in this part of the country for six months. Consequently, many people are dying of _____.
b There has been no rain in this part of the country for six months. Consequently, many people are dying of thirst.

8 a In spite of the fantastic _____, Ruritania is not a very popular place for tourists.
b In spite of the fantastic climate, Ruritania is not a very popular place for tourists.

E – *It*

Example: Many people do not like American pronunciation, but *it* is difficult to understand why.
Problem: Does this mean that American pronunciation is difficult to understand? If not, what does *it* mean?

We said in unit 4 that *it* is used in two ways in English:
(i) in certain fixed phrases like *It's raining.*
or *It's six o'clock.*
(ii) to refer to another word or thing, one which has usually come before: The chair was very expensive – it cost £6000. *It* refers to *chair*.

But there is another important use, which can confuse students:

(iii) *It* is very difficult to speak Chinese.

This really means:
   To speak Chinese is very difficult.
or Speaking Chinese is very difficult.

This form, *It is* + adjective + *to* + VERB, is very common.

Activity 11.5

Look at these three sentences:
a It's six o'clock.
b The chair was very expensive – it cost £6000.
c It is very difficult to speak Chinese.

Now look at the following sentences or extracts. In all of them, the word *it* appears. Are the sentences like a, b, or c above? Write a, b, or c in the box after each sentence and, if it is b, indicate with a circle and an arrow (as in 1) the word or phrase which it refers to.

1 Last night, we went to a new (play) at the Criterion Theatre. I didn't understand (it) very much! [b]

2 It's difficult to find a taxi at this time of night. [c]

3 We don't need to take an umbrella. It's always hot and sunny on the coast at this time of year. [a]

4 It's never easy to analyse people's behaviour. ☐

5 In August 1986, our firm changed owners. Before, it was owned by IBM. ☐

6 I didn't like the situation, and it was late at night by now. ☐

7 Last week, I read *War and Peace* again. It's a book we have all heard of, but few of us have read. ☐

8 We bought a very large Christmas tree, but it was impossible to get it through the door! ☐

9 You may find this exercise easy, but I can't do it! ☐

Activity 11.6
Read this description of an old lady, and decide what the circled words refer to. Use arrows to indicate, as in the first example.

Mrs Burningham was a strange character. (She) lived with her dog Timmy in a cottage in Putney. (It) was small and white, on the corner of Mansell Street and Common Road. (She) liked the house very much, I remember.

Her husband died in 1972 and Mrs Burningham was very sad – she loved (him) fondly – but she decided to stay in Putney. One day, about three years after (this), her son and daughter-in-law came to see her. (They) came nearly every week, but there was something different this time. They brought some documents in a black briefcase, and wanted the (old lady) to look at (them).

These documents gave the house to the children, and then Mrs Burningham could move into an old people's home nearby, (which) was very nice and comfortable, (they) said. But she didn't want to. She said (it) had a bad reputation.

Activity 11.7

Read this piece and answer the questions which follow.

The Ghost of Warmley

The ghost of Warmley is very famous. It lives in a small cottage in Pelham Street, in the centre of the city. The owner of the house is a young woman called Beth Mills, who has seen it three or four times. 'None of my neighbours in the road believe me,' she told me yesterday, 'but I've seen him, heard him, and even spoken to him! I call him Joe.'

In fact, Joe is not the only ghost in the town. There is another one which lives in the Lion Hotel in the High Street. But the only person who has seen it is a waiter, Mr Patrick Slugg, who has been working at the hotel for only six months. 'I believe this man was drunk at the time,' said the hotel's owner, Mrs Gloria Honeycandle, when I asked her about her mysterious guest. 'There are no ghosts in my establishment.'

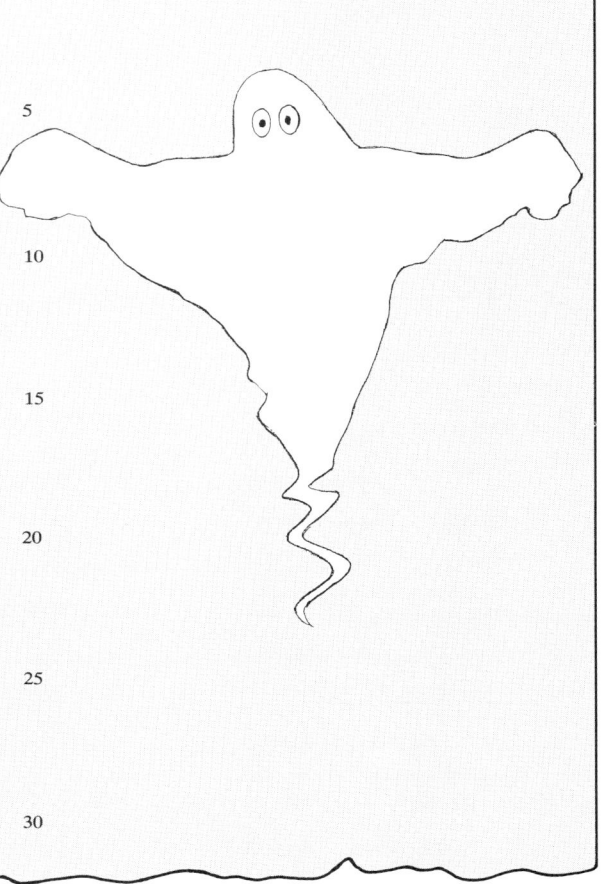

Line 2   What is IT? _the ghost_

Line 5   Which city? _____

Line 6   Which house? _____

Line 8   What is IT? _____

Line 10   What is THE ROAD? _____

Line 10   Who is SHE? _____

Line 12   Who is HIM? _____

Line 14   Who is Joe? _____

Line 16   What is THE TOWN? _____

Line 17   There is another what? _____

Line 21   Who or what is IT? _____

Line 23   Which hotel? _____

Line 24   Who is THIS MAN? _____

Line 28   Who is HER? _____

Line 28–9 Who is the MYSTERIOUS GUEST? _____

Line 30   What is MY ESTABLISHMENT? _____

Activity 11.8

Here is a short story in two parts. Put the sentences in the correct order. Write the letters in the spaces below each part:

PART ONE

a   'English?' he replied, 'Oh, new, new, very good. But don't tell the police.'
b   It was a beautiful hot summer's day.
c   So I went up to the man and asked him in English if they were new or second-hand.
d   One day, I went for a walk in the market.
e   They seemed very cheap – only about £30 in English money – and I needed a new camera.
f   The first thing I saw was a man selling Nikon cameras.

   1 _____ 2 _____ 3 _____ 4 _____ 5 _____
   6 _____

PART TWO

a   I walked back to my hotel and, very pleased with my morning's work, I opened the box.
b   So I gave him the money and he was just counting it when suddenly another man came up to him shouting, 'Police! Police!'
c   Inside there was a large stone!
d   After he said this, I realised at once that the cameras were stolen.
e   Immediately, the man folded up his small table, gave me the box with the camera in it and ran off.
f   This worried me a bit, but they were only £30...!

   1 _____ 2 _____ 3 _____ 4 _____ 5 _____
   6 _____

Discuss: Which words did you use to order the story? Write the words here:

_____
_____
_____
_____
_____

UNIT 12

Skimming and Scanning (2)

Students often want to understand everything when they are reading in a foreign language. This is quite natural, and sometimes even necessary. But when you read your own language, you often find certain words, phrases or even a whole article difficult (perhaps because the article is about a subject you do not know much about, or because it uses difficult or obscure language).

However, this does not mean that you stop reading the article or book, or that you go immediately to the dictionary. Usually, you continue reading in order to get the information you want. In this unit, you are going to read some passages which contain some difficult language, because for the most part they come from real English sources. Don't worry! As in unit 5, we will only be interested in extracting some of the information from a passage, and not in understanding everything.

Activity 12.1

Imagine you have arrived in England and you decide to go to Scotland. You look at an article 'Your Journey to Scotland': what information do you expect to find? For example, write down the possible ways of getting to Scotland (bus, train, etc.):

___

Now look at the article for ten seconds. How many of these ways does it talk about?

Now imagine that you want to travel to Edinburgh first. You have not yet decided how to travel. Write down a list of questions about the journey. (We have given you the first.)

How far is Edinburgh from London?

___
___
___
___

Now read the article quickly, and write down answers to your questions. If the answer is not there, write 'Don't know'. Do not worry about difficult words.

/94/

YOUR JOURNEY TO SCOTLAND

Your travel agent will provide full details of the various ways of travelling to Scotland. In addition to a variety of tour operators offering travel-inclusive packages, travelling north to Scotland by scheduled road, rail or air services is very simple.

By air

From London Heathrow, take advantage of the British Airways Shuttle to Edinburgh (leaving every two hours) or Glasgow (leaving every hour). These flights operate a 'turn up and take off' system, that is, there is no booking but you are guaranteed a seat for the one hour's flying time. British Caledonian, British Midland, Air UK and Dan Air also fly to Scottish destinations both from London and other English airports. Stand-by tickets are offered. You will find a convenient coach service between Glasgow Airport and the city centre, similarly between Edinburgh and its airport, as well as a feeder coach running Edinburgh/Edinburgh Airport/Glasgow/Prestwick.

By road

There are good motorway connections from both the north and south of England, as well as Wales. The M1/M6 is the quickest, though the A1 also allows a direct route. Edinburgh and Glasgow are around 400 miles (650 kilometres) from London, so allow a very comfortable 8 hours (including stops) – though remember Scotland starts at the Border! You can easily deduct an hour or two from the estimate if you want to take advantage of the plentiful accommodation on the Scottish side of the border.

By train

Modern and comfortable, British Rail Inter-City can take you from London to Edinburgh (depart King's Cross) or Glasgow (depart Euston) in about 5 hours. In addition there are both direct departures or convenient connections to Scotland from all other parts of the rail network. Overnight sleeper connections from London and Bristol operate to Edinburgh, Glasgow, Dundee, Perth, Aberdeen, Inverness, while taking your car on Motorail from London or Bristol is another travel option.

By bus

Long-distance coaches are often the cheapest way of travelling to Scotland. Scottish Omnibuses, Cotters, Stagecoach and other operators offer a regular service from London and other English departure points, in luxury vehicles offering the best of on-board entertainment and refreshments.

Distances in miles (kilometres)

	London		Bristol		Manchester		Newcastle	
Jedburgh	330	(531)	344	(554)	171	(275)	58	(93)
Gretna Green	311	(500)	287	(462)	129	(208)	67	(108)
Berwick	334	(537)	348	(560)	192	(309)	63	(101)
Glasgow	397	(639)	373	(600)	215	(346)	148	(238)
Edinburgh	378	(608)	373	(600)	215	(346)	110	(177)
Aberdeen	503	(809)	493	(793)	340	(547)	235	(378)
Inverness	536	(862)	539	(867)	373	(600)	268	(431)
John o'Groats	661	(1063)	653	(1050)	500	(804)	394	(634)

Activity 12.2

The following people have asked you to suggest a restaurant in Sandford. Read the descriptions of the people and then choose a restaurant for them from the Sandford restaurant guide.

1 *Mary and Jonathan Arnold (aged 29 and 27)*

Mary and Jonathan have been married for one year. They are going to celebrate their wedding anniversary on Friday 1st July and they would like you to recommend a romantic restaurant with good food. They do not like Indian food, and as it is a special occasion they can spend a lot of money.

I recommend _____

2 *Alan Simms (aged 19)*

Alan is a student at Sandford Art College. He lives 10 miles from Sandford and he attends college from 9.00 to 5.00 every day from Monday to Friday. He is looking for a cheap restaurant where he can have lunch.

I recommend _____

3 *Mr and Mrs Jones (aged 51 and 53)*

Mr and Mrs Jones have recently had a wonderful holiday in France, and they especially enjoyed French cooking. They are looking for a restaurant where they can go with their friends, Mr and Mrs Alders, who would also like to try out French food.

I recommend _____

4 *Maria Stewart (aged 21)*

Maria and her friends usually go straight from work to the cinema on Friday evenings. They would like to find a restaurant where they can buy some food to take home after they have been to the cinema.

I recommend _____

5 *Mikhail Andropov (aged 54)*

Mikhail is a business man from Leningrad. He is coming to Sandford next Thursday to discuss the possibility of a trade agreement with a local company. You have to take him out after the meeting. He would like to try traditional English food.

I would take him to _____

Sandford Restaurant Guide

FIELD'S
16 Church Row
Tel: 441–6793

A wide-ranging English menu, including beef braised with beer, Lancashire hotpot, Melton Mowbray pie, and cucumber and Stilton mousse. Most dishes are served with a baked potato and side salad, and to follow there is an assortment of English puddings, including spotted dick with custard. Crowded at weekends, but good value on weekdays.

Average meal for 2 – £24.00, wine from £7.00

Closed on Tuesdays

LA DOLCE VITA
15 St. Stephen's Rd.
Tel: 235–6841

One of the most recent Italian restaurants to spring up in this part of town, la Dolce Vita offers Italian cooking at its best. Try the spaghetti with salmon and caviar or the seafood risotto, followed by the spezzatino di vitello with mushrooms. The zabaglione is superb. Booking is essential – prices above average, but worth it.

Average meal for 2 – £35.00, wine from £8.00

Closed on Tuesdays

THE STANDARD
121 Park Way
Tel: 994–3872

Indian food at its best – and the prices are very reasonable. There is a wide range of curries, from a fairly mild Kashmiri rogan josh to a fiery pork vindaloo. Also specialises in vegetarian cooking – try their onion or aubergine bhajees.

Average meal for 2 – £18.00, wine £5–7.00

Closed on Mondays

TIMI'S CHINESE
21 King Street
Tel: 783–8822

This restaurant, with its typical oriental decor and excellent service, provides an ideal setting for a romantic candle-lit evening for two. The menu highlights such specialities as won ton soup, spinach and bean-curd soup and duck with Chinese mushrooms. Seating for only 25, and it is popular, so be sure to book at least 24 hours in advance.

Average meal for 2 – £20.00, wine £6.00

Closed on Fridays

SEAVIEW HOTEL
The Parade, Northwick Rd.
Tel: 554–6129

A choice of venues here: the newly decorated *Cocktail Bar* is an ideal place to start your evening, providing an exotic variety of cocktails to suit all tastes (and pockets). The *Fontana Restaurant* on the first floor provides a standard menu of prawn cocktail, steak and salad, with ice-cream or apple pie to follow. Good value if slightly monotonous.
   And in the *Lounge Bar* you can relax over a cup of coffee and an after dinner drink from the well-stocked range of liqueurs.

Fixed price menu for 1 in the Fontana – £10.50
Wine – £7.00

Restaurant only closed on Mondays

THE GRAND
Redham Road
Tel: 101–8876

Very much in the French tradition, the dining-room at the Grand caters for those with a little more money to spend. The handsome, courteous waiters are all French and serve an excellent variety of carefully prepared and served dishes, ranging from a soupe à l'oignon or escargots to coq au vin or filet au poivre vert. (Special lunch-time menu available on request.)

Average meal for 2 – £30.00, wine – £7–10.00

THE BURGER BAR
10 Market Place
Tel: 943–1269

A popular hamburger bar with a sit-down restaurant and also take-away facilities. Ideal for a snack after an evening out. Try their hamburgers with one of the interesting fillings available – tandoori tomato or blue cheese and chives to mention only two.

Standard burger with cheese – £1.75

Closed on Mondays

MARKET CAFÉ
14 Market Street
Tel: 562–9111

This self-service restaurant provides both hot and cold meals. The menu changes every day and includes salads, soups, quiches and pies. A good range of sweets, from a delicious fruit salad to home-made apple pie and custard or chocolate mousse. Recommended for students and those on a strict budget.

Average meal for 1 – £2.50

Closed on Sat. evening and Sunday

Activity 12.3

Read the short newspaper articles on the left and decide which of the three summaries a, b or c best sums it up.

1. Summer came early to Middlesbrough yesterday, as temperatures shot up to 22°C (71°F), a record for March. But local NFU agent Jim Wilkes says it could be bad news for farmers – 'The crops will think it's summer,' he told our reporter, 'and start sprouting four weeks before time.'

   a It is hotter than usual in Middlesbrough, and the farmers are pleased.
   b It is hotter than usual in Middlesbrough, and the farmers are worried.
   c It is colder than usual in Middlesbrough, and the farmers are worried.

2. The death toll of the Burnside train crash rose to four yesterday when John Phillips, 32, of Petersville, died in Wallsend Hospital. Another six people are still on the danger list. Mr Phillips, an electrical engineer, leaves a wife and two children.

   a Ten people have died in the crash, including John Phillips.
   b Four people have died in the crash, including John Phillips.
   c John Phillips, his wife and children all died in the crash.

3. Prospects for a US–USSR summit brightened yesterday when the White House spokesman Graham Torques announced that the Secretary of State Ronald Kistold would meet the Russian foreign minister Yevkedy Yankitov in Geneva in March. The two superpowers have not met at ministerial level since the abortive Reykyavik meeting two years ago. 'Maybe this time we can make some progress,' said an obviously delighted Mr Torques.

   a Relations between the USA and USSR are better.
   b Relations between the USA and USSR are worse.
   c Relations between the USA and USSR are the same.

Activity 12.4

Read the film reviews on the left and answer the questions on the right. Don't worry if you don't understand every word.

FILMS OF THE WEEK

LETTER TO BREZHNEV

This original and spontaneous movie, filmed entirely in Liverpool, is the story of two girlfriends, Alexandra Pigg and Margi Clarke, who come from a lower-middle-class background, and their encounter with two Russian sailors disembarked in the city. One of the girls falls for her comrade, who invites her back to Russia. Against opposition from family and friends, she finally decides to go. The film's main quality is its balance of entertainment and irony, with good performances from the central quartet, especially Pigg and Clarke.

A DOG IN HAND

This film has been an enormous success in Germany – showing how German cinema has lost its serious image and can now produce comedies to rank with the Americans. The story is of a small dog which captures the heart of three hard-boiled business men in Frankfurt: we watch them first try to sell the animal, then try to kill it, then finally fall in love with it. A lot of laughs, some good acting, but don't expect anything deep.

HEARTACHE

Director John Wills is well-known for his horror epics like *The Touch*, so this story, a romance set in a glossy, yuppified New York, is a real change. At the end of the film, however, you feel like you've been eating sugar continuously for a week – the encounters between the two central figures Jayne and Sean are trite and embarrassing, and the acting is awful. Some of the dialogue is good but, overall, the film is boring and sentimental. Wills should go back to horror!

Letter to Brezhnev:
1 The film is
   a a horror film
   b a love story
   c a political thriller
2 The review is
   a positive
   b negative
   c neither positive nor negative

A Dog in Hand:
3 The film is
   a philosophical
   b comic
   c serious

Heartache:
4 This is
   a a horror film
   b a romance
   c a documentary about sugar
5 The review is
   a positive
   b completely negative
   c mostly negative

Activity 12.5

Often the gist of an article is contained in the first and last paragraphs, or even the first and last sentences. (The others usually give more detailed information.) Read the title and first and last paragraphs/sentences of these articles. Can you find out what the articles are about? Discuss with your partner and your teacher.

THE BRAIN DRAIN

An American agency has been set up in London to try to 'steal' British science professors and teachers for US universities.

'The great advantage British academics have is that they speak the English language.'

NEW JOBLESS HIGH

The Government was attacked from all sides yesterday as the unemployment figures for March were published.

'This Government has no heart,' said Mrs Brian.

CRISIS IN FLORENCE

JUST by Kennyburger, Florence's newest fast food restaurant, a group of young tourists are throwing Coke cans and plastic cups into the river Arno.

'Someone must stop mass tourism destroying the places we love.'

LOVE IN THE STREET

When factory worker Pat Smith left home to go to work last Friday, she had no idea it was going to be a very special day for her.

The couple haven't decided on a honeymoon destination yet. 'Bermuda would be nice,' admitted Bob, 'but a bit expensive for us!'

THROAT OP FOR DAVID

Top pop singer Frank David will have throat surgery next week, and has cancelled all his 1989 performances.

Lindy Parks said the singer had asked the hospital's identity to be kept secret.

SWEETNESS AND LIGHT IN BERLIN

Productions at the Berlin Neutheater have tended to be dark, gloomy, tragic affairs in the past – like last year's *Hell and Heaven* directed by Klaus Vogel. But the new show there *A Little Bit of Gold* is in a completely different mould.

As director Schlesinger rightly says, if the audience doesn't enjoy itself, it won't come back.

Activity 12.6

Finally, here is an activity to practise both skimming and scanning.

Before you read, answer these questions:
1. What are the French famous for?
2. Have you ever eaten French food? What did you think of it?

Now look at the title:

French chefs get a taste for English

Do you know what a *chef* is? Can you guess?
What do you think the article is about?

Now look at the first and last sentences:

THE language of tomorrow's kitchen will not be French but English.

Today, if you cannot speak English, you cannot become a leader.'

Which of the following three sentences best summarises the content of the article?
a The best chefs nowadays are English, not French.
b Menus in France will now be printed in English.
c Chefs must speak English to communicate with other chefs.

Before you read the article in full, write down ten or twelve words you expect to read in it:

_____   _____   _____   _____
_____   _____   _____   _____
_____   _____   _____   _____

Now read the article. Read it quite quickly, and do not spend too much time thinking about difficult words. Look for the general sense of the article.

French chefs get a taste for English

By John Izbicki in Paris

1 THE language of tomorrow's kitchen will not be French but English. This surprising resolution was taken yesterday by a congress of leading French chefs.

2 Forty of the country's *Maîtres-Cuisiniers*, who for the past three days have been discussing policy at Clermont-Ferrand in the Auvergne, decided that their one big regret in life was their joint inability to speak English.

3 Would it mean that, in future, menus at some of the finest restaurants in the world might reject such popular dishes as *Boeuf Bourgignon*, *Profiterolles de lapereau au miel* and *Coq au Vin* and serve instead the more prosaic Beef Stew, Rabbit Pie with Honey and Chicken Casserole?

4 One of the attending 'mastercooks' looked suitably horrorstruck. '*Pas du tout*,' he replied, shaking his head so vigorously that his chef's hat was almost dislodged.

5 'English need not necessarily become the language of our dishes, but it is without any doubt the language of communication,' said M Jean-Yves Bathe, whose restaurant, the Clos St-Pierre at Clermont-Ferrand, has just one star in the Michelin Guide.

6 He explained: 'Our greatest cuisines are now not only run by French chefs, but also by British chefs, German chefs, American and Japanese chefs. What is the one language they have in common? Why, English, of course. I never learned English, but I shall be taking lessons as soon as I am able,' he said.

7 However, French remained the language spoken during their closing dinner – a sumptuous feast prepared and served by Master Chef Gilbert Vacher at the Chateau de Ravel, one of the finest castles in the Auvergne.

8 Last night, M Paul-Louis Meissonnier, president of the Association of Maîtres-Cuisiniers de France and among France's greatest chefs, said: 'The French have always taught the rest of the world how to eat and throughout the 19th century London's palaces, including Buckingham Palace, and the best hotels, had French chefs.

9 'Now, the best cuisine is beginning to disappear from the fine hotels and palaces abroad. Why? Because the chefs do not speak English. Today, if you cannot speak English, you cannot become a leader.'

Which of the three summarising sentences did you choose? After having read the article, have you changed your mind?

How many of the words you listed did you find in the piece? Now read the article again. Underneath, you will find some questions about it. Write down the number of the paragraph where the answer to the question can be found.

1 Where did the meeting take place? ☐
2 Does Mr Bathe speak English? ☐
3 Who is Mr Paul-Louis Meissonnier? ☐
4 What is the English name for coq au vin? ☐
5 Who prepared the closing dinner? ☐
6 Why is the best cuisine beginning to disappear from fine hotels and palaces? ☐
7 What has got one star? ☐
8 What do you need to become a leader? ☐
9 Who is going to take English lessons soon? ☐
10 How many people attended the meeting? ☐

UNIT 13

Looking for Detailed Information (2)

In unit 12, we saw that we can often find the information we need in a text without understanding everything. However, sometimes we need to read more carefully because we have to understand in more detail. This unit will give you practice in this.

Activity 13.1
You have arrived in Scotland and you want to visit several different places. Look at the article (do not read it!). There are five sections:
a   an introduction
b   By air
c   By rail
d   By road
e   By sea (and lochs, too)

Now look at these questions and write the title of the section of the article where you will look for the answers to these questions:

1   Is there a bus service between the small villages in Scotland? Section _____

2   Is it possible to fly to the islands near Scotland? Section _____

3   Where can I get more information about boat-trips in Scotland? Section _____

4   Where can I see old steam trains still running? Section _____

Now look at these four questions again, look through the article as quickly as possible, and write the answers below:

1   _____
2   _____
3   _____
4   _____

/102/

TRAVELLING AROUND

A good road network, a rail system that takes you far north and far west, an efficient inter-island ferry fleet and a comprehensive island-hopping air service, are all available to ensure you reach your chosen destination in good time to enjoy your Scottish stay.

By air

Air Ecosse, Loganair and British Airways connect not only the main towns but also the Western Isles and the Orkneys and Shetlands. Flying is clearly the most effective way, on a tight schedule, to visit some of the more remote and beautiful parts of Scotland. A British Airways **Highland Rover** ticket gives 14 days unlimited flights both on the mainland and the islands.

By rail

In addition to the main Inter-City routes, with frequent services connecting Edinburgh, Glasgow, Stirling, Perth, Dundee, Aberdeen, Inverness (and stations between), Scotland is fortunate to possess lines that run through the very best of Highland scenery. Aberdeen–Inverness, Glasgow–Stranraer, Glasgow–Oban, Perth–Inverness are splendid journeys, likewise the famous Kyle Line which runs from Inverness across Scotland to Kyle of Lochalsh – after which a five minute ferry journey takes you to the mountainous island of Skye. And a very special experience awaits you on the West Highland line that runs from Glasgow up to Fort William and on to Mallaig. During the summer there are regular steam-hauled services between Fort William and Mallaig, with preserved locomotives and coaches authentically decorated in the style of an earlier age – a must for all railway enthusiasts! Full details from British Rail stations. Special day tours are also operated by BR from most major towns, full details from the Chief Passenger Manager, British Rail, Scottish Region, Buchanan House, 58 Port Dundas Road, Glasgow G4 0HG or tel. 041–332 9811.

British Rail make it easy to see the best of Scotland with their Freedom of Scotland tickets – 7 or 14 day unlimited travel over the network, starting any time. Enquire at a British Rail station for further details. **Railcards** also cut the cost of travel for young person, family or senior citizen, then take advantage of a variety of half-price fare combinations. Local stations both in the UK and Europe can also supply details of **Inter-Rail Pass** – a discount travel card for the under 26s.

By road

Travelling by bus often represents the most economical way of seeing Scotland, and sampling local life. A variety of areas, large and small, offer special deals for visitors. Both Edinburgh and Glasgow, for example, offer a variety of special concessions for visitors, as well as tours in and beyond the city.

For the Highlands and Islands, that is, most of Scotland north and west of the central belt, a **Travelpass** offers unlimited travel on train, bus and ferry services within the area. Full information from **Highlands and Islands Information Services, Main Street, Golspie, Sutherland, tel. (040 83) 3871**.

Finally, remember that many rural areas also operate a post bus service, carrying small numbers of passengers in addition to mail. Full information from local post offices or the Head Post Office, Edinburgh.

By sea (and lochs, too)

For cruises, or island hopping, as well as special packages such as Hebridean Drive Away, Mini Cruises from Oban, Come for a Sail on the Clyde, full details of concessions, dates and prices are available from **Caledonian MacBrayne Limited, The Ferry Terminal, Gourock, Renfrewshire, tel. (0475) 33755**. Other island ferry details from Western Ferries, P & O Ferries, B. T. A. and local tourist information centres.

Now look at this form and fill in the missing information from the article:

TRAVELLING IN SCOTLAND

Main airlines operating in Scotland

_____

_____

_____

Inclusive travel tickets:

    a Highland Rover – operated by _____

           duration _____

    b Freedom of Scotland – operated by _____

           duration _____

    c Travelpass – Information from _____

Scenic railway lines:

Aberdeen – Inverness

Glasgow – _____

_____ – Oban

_____ – Inverness

_____ – _____ (Kyle Line)

For information on cruises and travel between islands, telephone

_____

Activity 13.2

Read the letters, the birthday card and the report, and use the information to complete the curriculum vitae.

CURRICULUM VITAE

Name: EDWARD STOCKER

Address:

Age:

Present Occupation:

Marital Status:

Education and Qualifications

3 GCEs grade B

2

Experience

1970 to 1975

1975 to 1978

1978 to date

Referees

1 Mr John Sayles,
    The Lodge,
    4 Milton Drive,
    London N8

2 Mr Frank Partridge,

> We spoke to Mr Ralph Edward Stocker, the other candidate, at length. He has very long experience, having worked as a salesman or sales manager since he left school at 16. Unfortunately, he has no qualifications apart from 5 GCEs grades B and D, and we feel he may be a little under-qualified for such a demanding and responsible post

---

76A Wilton Road,
Salisbury,
Wilts

4 March 19--

Dear Sirs,

I am writing to apply for the position as sales manager, as advertised in 'Tyre Monthly' of 12 January.

As you can see from my enclosed c.v., I have a good deal of experience in both selling tyres and in managing a team of salesmen in the field. I started my career in 19-- with Dunelli Ltd., where I worked for five years as a salesman, before moving to Fireyear for three years. I then moved back to Dunelli, where I have been ever since as sales manager.

HAPPY BIRTHDAY

Ralph

Don't forget – life begins at 35!

from your ever-loving wife Dulcie

---

41 Bond Street,
Norwich.

4/2/--

Dear Ralph,

   Thanks for your letter of 12th January. Of course, I'd be pleased to be a referee for you. Good luck with your application.

   Yours,

   Frank

Activity 13.3

Read the extract from the detective's notebook, and put in the names on the plan of the dinner table.

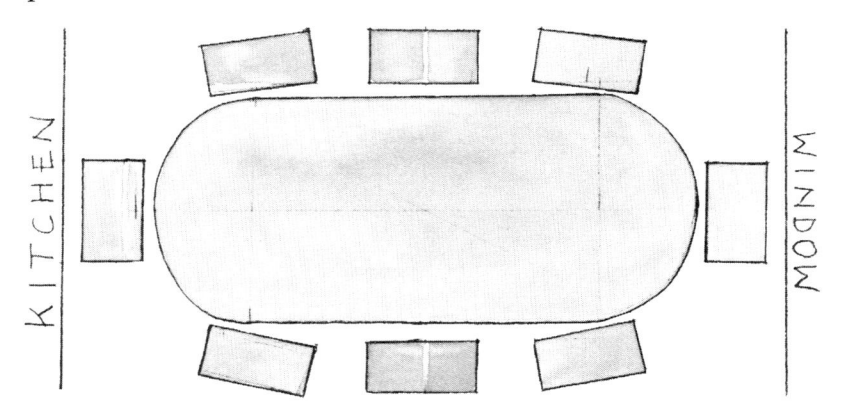

According to the interviews I conducted after the incident, the position of the dinner guests seems clear. As hosts, Mr and Mrs Black were at the ends of the table. Mrs Black normally sits at the end near the kitchen, but on this occasion Mr Black had a little backache, and asked not to sit near the window. Dennis Black, the son, was sitting on his mother's left, and next to him was his fiancée, Greta. Unfortunately, this meant Greta was opposite Paul, her old boyfriend, but it didn't seem to matter. Paul was more interested in the girl on his right, who was a Swedish writer called Ulmar (I think). The party was completed by Paul's sister Betty, who was next to Mr Black, and Ralph Johnson, who is reputed to be Mrs Black's lover.

Activity 13.4

Read the passage, and match the drawings with the bar-graphs. The first one has been done for you.

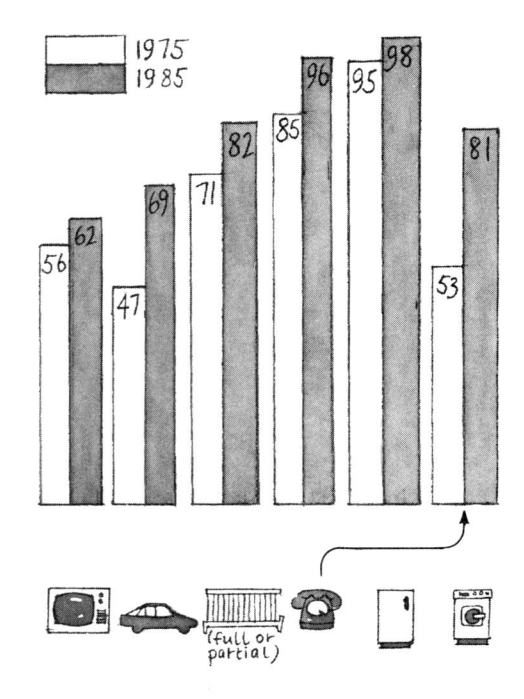

A survey carried out by the Department of Consumer Affairs shows that certain durable goods increased considerably their market penetration during the ten years between 1975 and 1985, whilst others remained almost static. The biggest increase was in the number of households with telephones, which rose from 53% in 1975 to 81% in 1985. The other 'big-riser' was central heating systems, which increased their percentage by 22% in the same ten years. Strangely, of the six goods in the survey (TVs, telephones, cars, central heating, fridges and washing machines), cars are now the least popular, only 62% of households having them. It's another strange fact that more households have TVs than fridges, with 98% and 96% respectively. Presumably, English clothes are now much cleaner, with washing machines up from 71% to 82%.

Activity 13.5

You are the editor of a local newspaper in Birmingham in England. One of your reporters has written an article about a local writer, Joanna Growles, based on an interview he had with her; but, unfortunately, the reporter made a number of mistakes in the article. Read the interview and the article, and complete the memo to the reporter.

Interview

Reporter: *Ms Growles, can you tell me when you started writing?*
Joanna Growles: Well, I wrote quite a lot at school, poetry, short stories, that kind of thing. But the first thing to be published was a story called 'Pride' which came out in 1979, the year after I left school.
Rep: *You went to Newcastle University, didn't you? What was that like?*
JG: Well, I enjoyed it, though I was so busy writing that I didn't have much time for studying or anything like that.
Rep: *And after university, you produced six novels in ten years . . .*
JG: Well, in fact, at least two of those six I wrote during my time at Newcastle, but they only came out afterwards. I had a novel called *Excessive Measures* which was published in 1984, which was quite successful, and so it got much easier after that.

Rep: *What is your attitude to writing? Do you sit down at 9 o'clock in the morning and write until 5 in the evening?*
JG: Absolutely not! I wish I could. I mean I often sit down at 9, and don't know what to write! I usually have to wait for inspiration, and if it comes in the middle of the night, well then, I write in the middle of the night!
Rep: *You've lived in this area all your life. Do you see yourself as a Birmingham writer above all?*
JG: In fact, it is not true I've lived here all my life. I was born in Birmingham, and I lived here till I was three, but until about ten years ago I lived in Canterbury in Kent. I only moved back to Birmingham because my ex-husband got a job here. He now lives in London, and I'm still here! I don't mind Birmingham at all – it's a very dynamic place, and the people are much kinder and friendlier than in other places. But I think I've really stayed here because I'm too lazy to move.
Rep: *Any plans for the future?*
JG: I've just finished my first play *Overnight Success*, which we hope to put on some time. And I've nearly finished my eighth novel, which will be in the shops next year.

OVERNIGHT SUCCESS

Peter Douglas talks to local writer Joanna Growles

Novelist Joanna Growles is probably Birmingham's most famous writer: she was born here, and has lived here all her life except for the time when she was at university at Canterbury.

She started writing when she was at school, and her first published work, a short story called "Pride" dates from that time. Her first novel, *Excessive Measures*, was published in 1974, and since then she has never looked back.

She reveals that all her writing takes place in the middle of the night (but it doesn't seem to worry her husband, who also lives in Birmingham). She says she only stays in the city because she's 'too lazy to move', although she likes the people.

Her new novel *Overnight Success* is out next year. Good luck, Ms Growles!

MEMO
From: the Editor
To: Peter Douglas

There were a number of errors in the article about Joanna Growles:

1. She hasn't lived here all her life.
2.
3.
4.
5.
6.
7.

Please put them right!

Activity 13.6

Have you got a pet at home (for example, a dog or a cat)? How do you look after it?

You are going to read a piece about caring for and looking after pets, especially cats and dogs.

Before you read the piece, imagine a friend of yours has just bought a dog, and asks you for some advice about how to keep it. What would you say? Write down four 'golden rules':

1 _____
2 _____
3 _____
4 _____

Now read the twelve rules, and tick (✓) the ones that you predicted above.

12 steps to good pet care

By observing these 12 basic rules, you will help to make life easier for you, for your pet and for everybody concerned.

1. Train your dog in elementary obedience so that it is under control at all times.
2. Feed your dog or cat at regular times, and do not give titbits between meals.
3. Feed your dog or cat from its own dish, which must be kept apart from those of the human family, and washed up separately.
4. Keep your dog on a lead anywhere near a road, or where there are farm animals.
5. Do not allow your dog to foul buildings, pavements, lawns and gardens or open spaces, especially where children play.
6. Do not allow your dog to be noisy and disturb your neighbours.
7. Provide your dog or cat with its own bed. Don't let it sleep on yours.
8. Never take your dog into a food shop.
9. Keep your dog clean and regularly groomed. Your cat will also need grooming, particularly if it is a long-haired variety.
10. If you do not wish your dog to have puppies or your cat to have kittens, you should obtain advice from your veterinary surgeon.
11. Make proper arrangements for the care of your pet when you are going on holiday.
12. Register your pet as a patient and yourself as a client with a veterinary surgeon of your choice. Do not wait for an emergency.

Now look at the pictures on the facing page. In each one, a pet owner is either following or breaking one of the rules. Write the number of the rule in the box under the picture, and put a tick (✓) if he or she is following the rule, or a cross (X) if he or she is breaking it.

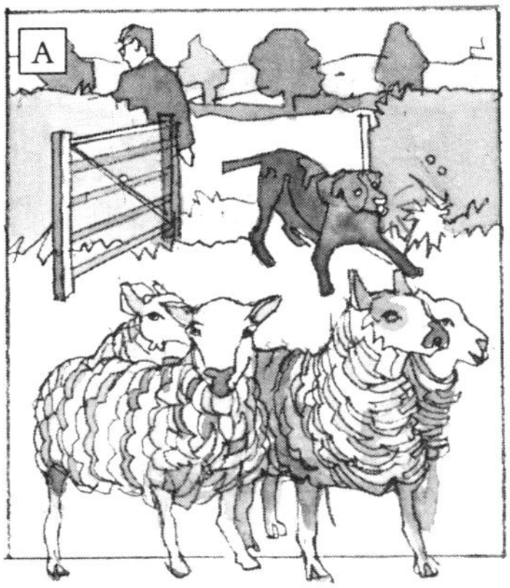
A

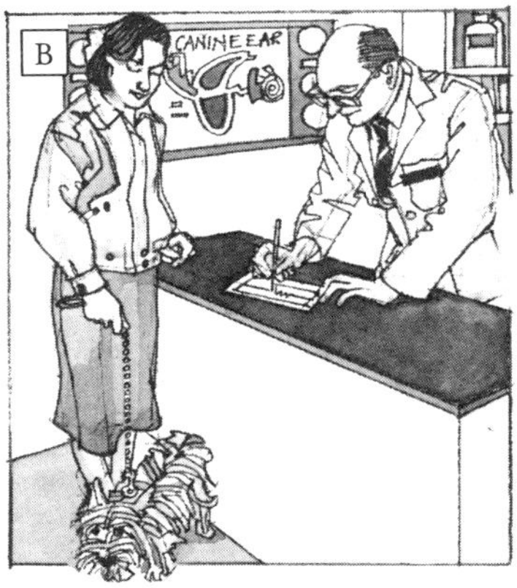
B
CANINE EAR

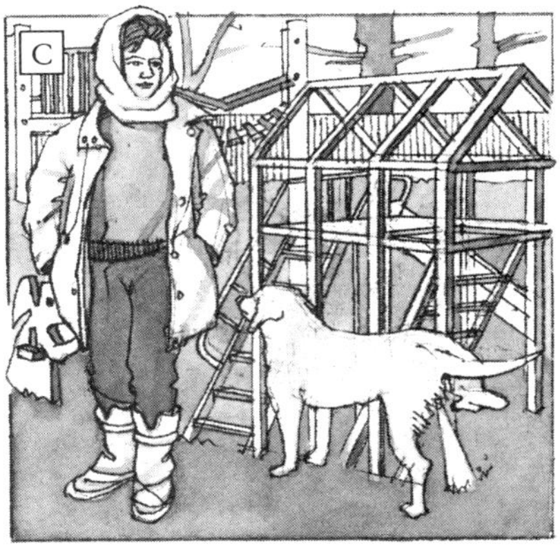
C

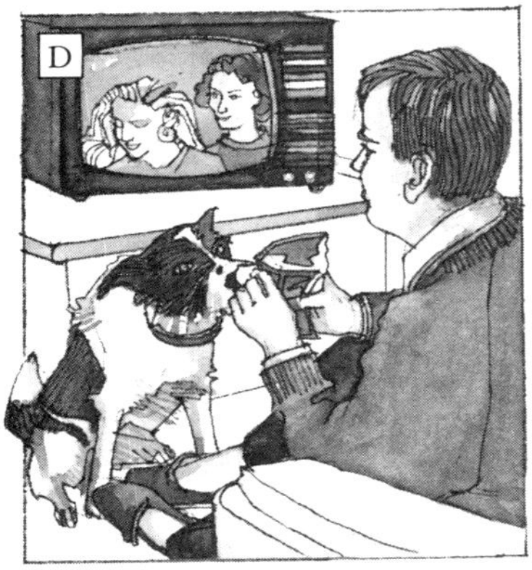
D

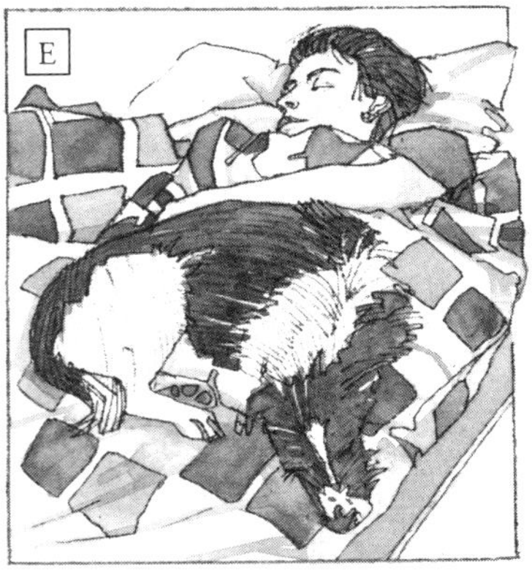
E

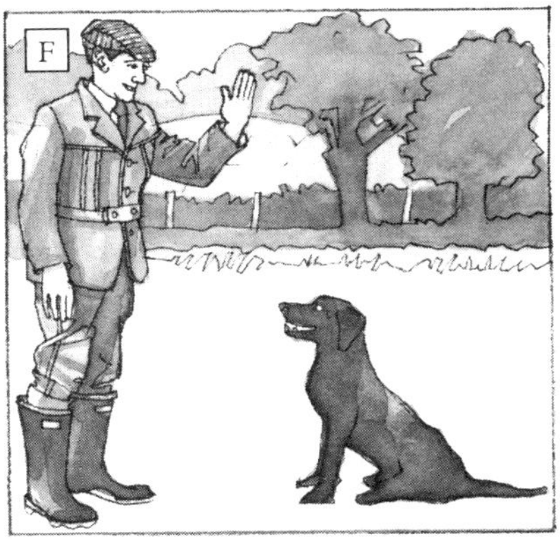
F

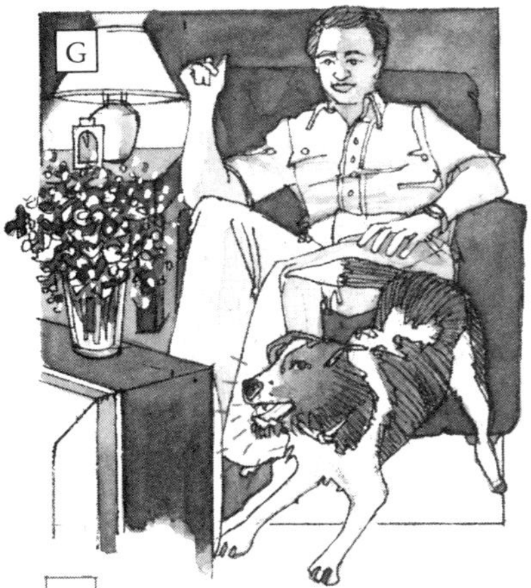
G

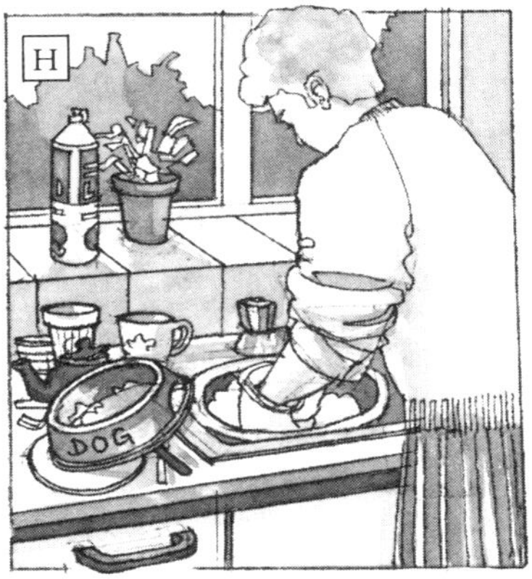
H
DOG

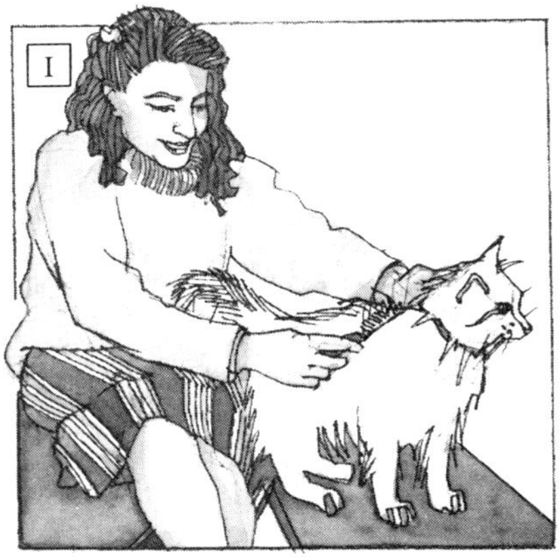
I

UNIT 14

Mixed Skills (2)

BUDAPEST

Activity 14.1

A Scanning

What do you know about Budapest? Look quickly through this passage and find the answers to these questions:

1. Which country is Budapest the capital of?
2. Which river is Budapest on?
3. How many people lived there in 1983?
4. Which is Budapest's busy season: spring, summer, autumn or winter?

---

a Budapest, the capital of Hungary, is situated on the River Danube, at the foot of the Buda Hills. The position of the city centre is 47°28'56"N and 19°08'10"E.

b Human settlements have existed in this region as far back as the Paleolithic Period. The Romans had a garrison here: the ruins can be seen at Obuda. During later periods the area was inhabited by the Huns, the Eastern Goths and others.

c In the reign of Kings Zsigmond and Matthias Corvinus, the city became famous, and a centre of European classical culture. From 1541 to 1686, it was under the rule of the Turks. Then, in the nineteenth century, a period of large-scale industrialisation, the three independent cities Pest, Buda and Obuda were unified as Budapest. World War II hit the city hard, but thanks to reconstruction, the city has become larger and more beautiful than ever before.

d The number of inhabitants in 1983 was 2,064,307. Its area is 525.6 square kilometres, of which 173.2 square kilometres are on the right bank of the Danube, and 352.4 on the left. The highest point above sea-level is Jànos-hegy, 527m.

e It is a unique feature of the capital that it is not only an industrial, economic and cultural centre, but also a health resort and spa. In Budapest there are 123 points where mineral and thermal waters come to the surface. These springs deliver 73 million litres of hot and warm water a day. The water is used to cure diseases of the bones.

f There are fine facilities for the visitor (the busiest period is between July and September). Hotels of all categories, inns, and private houses give a wide choice of accommodation. The famous Hungarian cuisine can be found in the large number of restaurants and bars in all parts of the city.

B Skimming:

Match these six titles with the six paragraphs:

1. Eating and Sleeping ☐
2. The last 450 years ☐
3. Facts and Figures ☐
4. Location ☐
5. Ancient History ☐
6. The Health-giving Waters ☐

/112/

C Guessing vocabulary from context:
Read the text about Budapest again. Find the words below (1–10) in the text and underline them. Then match the definitions on the right with the words on the left. Use the passage to help you to understand the words. Note that there are more definitions than words! The first one is done for you.

[c]	1	settlements	a	small hotel or place where you can stay
☐	2	garrison	b	big, extensive
☐	3	ruins	c	small towns and villages
☐	4	under the rule of	d	places where water comes out of the ground
☐	5	large-scale	e	a place where you keep money
☐	6	bank	f	a town where people who are ill go to get better
☐	7	health resort	g	the side of a river
☐	8	inns	h	buildings which are in bad condition because of their age
☐	9	cuisine	i	controlled by
☐	10	springs	j	strong
			k	a group of soldiers living in a town or city
			l	style of cooking

Activity 14.2

A Prediction
Look at the title and picture:

FUTONS

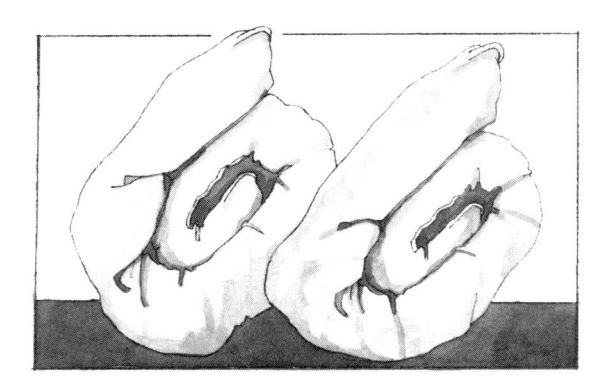

What is a futon? Can you guess from the picture?
Where do you think it comes from?
What do you think the article will be about?

B Skimming
Read the passage on p. 144 quickly (you have only 60 seconds!) and answer these questions:
1 What is a futon?
2 The *main* purpose of the article is
   a to give you information about the size and price of a futon
   b to tell you the good and bad things about a futon
   c both a and b

FUTONS

35 *Which?* readers changed their bed for a futon. This is what they reported:

A futon is a 3 inch thick cotton mattress (also available in 6 inch size). You can get futons made of other material, but readers preferred cotton ones.

The futon originally comes from Japan. The Japanese use it directly on the floor: during the day, it's folded away in a cupboard.

A futon here costs around £75 for a single, £95 for a double. You can buy a wooden base to raise it off the floor, or a base which lets you use your futon as a sofa as well as a bed.

Overall, most of our futon owners were happy and wouldn't go back to their old beds. The advantages were:
* space saving – good for a small bedsit or flat
* a convenient spare bed that you can move about easily
* firm – some readers with backache reported an improvement (but before deciding, talk to a doctor)
* less 'bouncing' when you get in and out of bed – a plus for light sleepers with restless partners
* no risk of children falling

The disadvantages were:
– difficult to roll and unroll every day because it's heavy (but you can leave it out if you've got space)
– frequent airing, turning and rolling to keep the futon smooth and dry
– as it's used on the floor, you may get draughts
– some discomfort (aches and pains) at first, because of the firmness
– possible problems for people who find it difficult to get up off a low bed

NB: if you use your futon on a base, some of these advantages and disadvantages may not apply.

Which? Verdict
By and large, our readers who had futons liked them. However, they are not suitable for everybody. If you can, try one for a few days before you buy.

C Scanning
Answer these questions as quickly as possible.
1 How thick is a futon?
2 Where does it come from?
3 Do you sleep on it?
4 How much do they cost?
5 Did the people who were trying them like them?

D Detailed information
Which of these people will probably like a futon? Tick (✓) yes or no.

		YES	NO
1	People with children		
2	People who don't like housework		
3	People with a small house		
4	People who have difficulty lifting things		
5	People who often have guests to stay		
6	People who like a high bed		
7	People with backache		
8	A wife who has a husband who moves a lot at night		

E Guessing vocabulary from context

Read the article again. Find the words below (1–10) in the text and underline them. Then match the definitions on the right with the words (1–10) on the left. Use the other words in the article to help you to understand the words – no dictionaries! The first one is done for you.

e	1	folded away	a	in general
☐	2	wooden	b	never still or quiet
☐	3	raise	c	air coming under the door
☐	4	overall	d	hard or quite hard
☐	5	improvement	e	put away/bent up to occupy a smaller space
☐	6	restless	f	right, appropriate
☐	7	roll	g	move from a lower level to a higher level
☐	8	draughts	h	make into a cylinder or ball
☐	9	firm	j	getting better
☐	10	suitable	k	made of wood

Activity 14.3

Read the following piece quickly, and decide which of these would be the better title for it:

THE FIVE SENSES or SEEING AND HEARING

Do you wear glasses? If you do, try this experiment: if you are wearing them at this moment, take them off. If you are not, put them on. Now, answer this question: can you *hear* better with them on or off?

A British scientist, who has been doing research into this area for many years, says you can hear better with your glasses on. Why should this be? Some people have suggested it is because you can lipread better with glasses. But no: it happens on the phone too. Others claim that the frames of the glasses push the ears forward so you can hear more easily. But no: it happens with contact lenses, as well.

Psychologists suggest two possible reasons: the first is that one part of the brain deals with information coming from the eye, a second with information coming from the ear; and a third which processes information from both. The idea is that when your glasses are off, the brain must cope with fuzzy images and so work harder, and so spend less time on the hearing.

But the most likely explanation is that since vision is the most important sense to us, when we are seeing well, we 'feel good' about our other senses.

/115/

A Finding your way around the text
What do the following words refer to?

line 3   them   line 21   it   line 31   both
line 13 this   line 27   second

B Guessing vocabulary from context
What do these words mean? (Choose between a or b)

1 research (line 10)   a studies   b surgical operations
2 lipread (line 16)   a kiss   b understand somebody by
                                                  looking at their lips
3 frames (line 19)   a the plastic or metal parts of glasses
                            b the glass part of glasses
4 contact lenses (line 22)
5 brain (line 25)

6 fuzzy (line 33)   a not clear   b very clear
7 likely (line 36)   a friendly   b probable

C Answer these questions:

1 Write in one sentence what the British scientist is saying.
   _____

2 What are the two explanations which the writer doesn't believe?
   _____
   _____

3 Why doesn't he believe them?
   _____
   _____

4 What are the other two explanations?
   _____
   _____

/116/

Activity 14.4

A Finding the order

Put these sentences in order to make a story. Note the words which helped you. The first one is done for you.

☐ During the interval, the audience and cast drank together in one of these.

☐ When we got home, we told all our friends about it.

[1] One afternoon, my husband and I wandered into a little Andalusian town in a romantic valley.

☐ We felt the same way: it was all so spontaneous.

☐ We walked around the picturesque streets and liked it so much we decided to come back in the evening.

☐ We sat down there, underneath the majestic walnut trees and watched all the old men sitting outside the cafés.

☐ They said the town was called San Dolosa and it was a famous Spanish tourist centre. It was like saying we had discovered Big Ben.

☐ At about 8.30, we came to the town square, where the locals were performing 'Carmen' in the open air.

☐ The opera started again, and the old man sitting next to me started to cry when the heroine died.

Write down here a list of the words which helped you:

_____
_____
_____

Now read the correct version on the next page and check your answer. Then answer the questions which follow it.

/117/

One afternoon, my husband and I wandered into a little Andalusian town in a romantic valley. We walked around the picturesque streets and liked it so much we decided to come back in the evening. At about 8.30, we came to the town square, where the locals were performing
5   'Carmen' in the open air. We sat down there, underneath the majestic walnut trees, and watched all the old men sitting outside the cafés.

During the interval, the audience and cast drank together in one of these. The opera started again, and the old man sitting next to me started to cry when the heroine died. We felt the same way: it was all so
10 spontaneous.

When we got home, we told all our friends about it. They said the town was called San Dolosa and it was a famous Spanish tourist centre. It was like saying we had discovered Big Ben.

B Finding your way around the text

line 3   What is *it*? _____
line 4   8.30 am or pm? _____
line 5   Where is *there*? _____
line 8   What are *these*? _____
line 8   Why *again*? _____
line 9   How did they feel? _____
line 11 What is *it*? _____
line 11 Who are *they*? _____

C Word-Guessing
Choose between a and b. Don't use a dictionary!

1 wander into (line 1)   a find accidentally
                              b walk around in
2 picturesque (line 2)   a modern
                              b pretty
3 majestic (line 5)   a small
                              b big
4 interval (line 7)   a break in the middle of a show
                              b the time when the sun goes down
5 spontaneous (line 10)   a unexpected and unplanned
                              b horrible
6 got (line 11)   a found
                              b arrived
7 discovered (line 13)   a found
                              b invented

Activity 14.5

The final passage in this book has a different kind of exercise. You are asked to give a personal reaction to what you read. First look at the photo:

What is your immediate reaction to this picture?
What country is it?
What do you think the words on the placard mean?
What do you think the piece you are going to read is about?

Now read the passage and answer the questions as they appear:

If you are reading this, the chances are that you live in one of the industrialised countries of the world. That means you are lucky.

    Why are you lucky?

You are lucky because you are rich. The industrialised countries between them possess 78% of all existing wealth. This means that the other countries (which are usually called the 'Third World') own about 22%, even though their population is about 76% of the world's total.

    What is your reaction to this information?

Of course, there are many people who live in the industrialised countries who are very concerned about this enormous disparity: most people give money at some time or other to help people in the poorer countries.

    What do you think of people who give money like this?

However, this fact may be part of the problem itself: the many organisations in the West who work to improve conditions in the Third World sometimes do more harm than good.

    Why do you think this is?

This is because these organisations (or *some* of them) are importing Western technology and aid into the underdeveloped countries: they have built dams, factories, airports and irrigation schemes. This has brought about two results.

    What are these results, do you think?

/119/

The first is that these poor countries become dependent on the richer countries – they need them more and more. Secondly, the importation of this kind of help has largely been based in the cities, causing a drift of population from the countryside to the towns.

> What do you think the effect of this is?

This has led to overcrowding and massive housing problems in the towns, and the depopulation and relative decline of the countryside.

> Is there an answer to this problem?
> Can you suggest one?

One possibility might be to encourage a different kind of technology,

> How would this technology be different?

which would be based more on local needs and local resources, without a large input of capital, and without requiring a high level of training. This would be based in the countryside, and not in the cities.

    In fact, in many countries this approach is already being tried. For example, farmers in Africa used to be given expensive tractors imported from England. These tractors required a skilled mechanic to repair them if they went wrong; also the spare parts which were needed had to be brought from England.

> What do you think happened to these tractors?

Of course, the first time the tractors broke down, they were left rusting in the fields. Nowadays, the approach might be to teach local people to build simple machines (such as ploughs) using simple, cheap, readily available materials which can easily be replaced. In this way, the local people learn to become independent of the West and Western technology. As the Chinese proverb says:
    'Give a man a fish and feed him for a day. Teach him how to fish and he'll feed himself for a lifetime.'

> What do you think this proverb means?
>
> What is your reaction to the whole passage?

Teacher's Notes and Key

Teacher's Notes

There are notes only for some of the activities; no notes are given where they are not necessary.

Unit 1

The exercises in this unit are not designed to improve the students' vocabulary, but to increase their capacity to guess meaning from context and form. Before you start, you should work through an example with the whole class. Write on the board: *I'm reading a really good novel at the moment*. Underline *novel*. Ask what they think it means. Encourage answers like *book, magazine, newspaper*. With the students, try to decide which of the three words is more likely and why. Explain that *reading* and *a really good . . .* are part of the context, and that the context is vital for guessing unfamiliar words. Provide other examples if necessary (but make sure the students do not already know the underlined word in the example).

You will probably need to point out that, in all these activities, the underlined word is more difficult than the others, and the students are not expected to know it.

Understanding a word from its context

Activity 1.1

Explain the word *italics* before starting the activity. It is strongly recommended that this activity (and all the others in this unit) is done in pairs.

Activity 1.2

Ask students to justify their choice (in English, if possible).

Activity 1.4

The students need to form only the base word (not all the missing forms).

Activity 1.5

This activity is more difficult, requiring the student to provide more language. However, encourage answers in English, even in monolingual classes: accept any answers which communicate the general meaning of the word.

Understanding a word from its form

This section is designed to show students that it is sometimes, but not always, possible to guess meaning from form.

If you have a monolingual class, you could introduce the activities by inventing a few words in their language that could be guessable from form (or get the students to do it).

Activity 1.7

Put the words *economist* and *pianist* on the board and indicate the –ist ending, and how it operates. The students should do the matching exercise without dictionaries.

Activity 1.8

The first part (eliciting *teacher, writer*, etc.) should be done with the students' books closed, while the teacher asks the questions. The students then read sentences 1–5 and decide if their guesses were right. (Beware! *cooker* is a machine for cooking.) Emphasise that they must always check their guesses from the sense. The students then move on to sentences 6–14.

Activity 1.9 (Compound Nouns)

Put examples on the board first and elicit possible meanings. Point out that the first part is a noun, but used as an adjective. Ask students to write definitions (preferably in English) for the compound nouns in the activity, then discuss with the whole class.

Unit 2

The purpose of this unit is to improve the students' capacity to make predictions about a text both before reading it and while doing so. Pictures, typeface, headlines, can all be used for this, and teachers are advised, before using any text with a class, to exploit these so-called extra-linguistic features to the full. If you have a monolingual class, bring in the morning paper in the students' own language; read out a few headlines, show them some photos (or both) and ask for predictions about the content.

As an introduction to the material in this unit, write the book-titles on page 15 on the board, and ask for predictions. Find out which of the titles interest which students.

Activity 2.1

Demonstrate to the class how newspapers are divided into sections (sports, arts etc.) according to content.

Activity 2.2

Do the same as in 2.1, but with summaries instead. As an introduction to more detailed prediction, put some newspaper or magazine titles on the board and ask the students to make lists of some words which might come up in the articles. If they find this too difficult, write up lists yourself (as on page 44) and ask students to tick the words which they think will occur.

Activity 2.3

This is not a writing exercise! Accept any answer which fits the title. (Monolingual classes could do it in their own language.) Do not worry about the grammar of their predictions, but only about their content. After they have read the text, ask the students which predictions were correct. This exercise should have helped with the difficult words – ask students to guess/estimate what they mean.

The remainder of page 18 can be worked through on the board or on the overhead projector.

Activity 2.4

One way of exploiting this activity might be to write all the students' suggestions on the board, and compare them with the originals: for 1, for example, most students will suggest a relative of some kind, which allows them to guess the rough meaning of *nephew*.

Activity 2.5

An overhead projector is highly recommended for this. You should cover the text so that the students can only see the first line ('My sister Jane...'). Then reveal the question. Ask students to write their answers and, when they have all thought about it, ask for the answers orally. You should get the names of jobs. Stress that the students do not have to guess the exact word (though they will get some satisfaction if they do) but any word which is logical in that position – for example, *postman, nurse, teacher*, etc.

Reveal the second line, and continue.

If you do not have an overhead projector, the students must cover the text themselves with a piece of paper, and move it down the page following your instructions. If they jump ahead, the point of the activity is lost.

Activities 2.6/2.7

Use the same technique as for 2.5. Ask the students to justify their answers.

Unit 3

Before starting this unit, ensure that all the students have access to a good monolingual dictionary (see page 22). If students have other dictionaries, such as the small pocket ones or dictionaries prepared for mother tongue English speakers, ask them to work through this unit and unit 10 using the recommended dictionaries, and then, on the basis of what they have learnt, to evaluate their own dictionaries. It is probably not a good idea to tell students that their own dictionaries are not good enough; it is better to let them find out for themselves that this is the case.

You should not let them use a bilingual dictionary, as they will not gain the intended benefit from the exercises.

Activity 3.1

It is important for all students to be thoroughly familiar with the English alphabet and to be able to find words quickly in their dictionaries. Parts i-iii are designed for students who do not use the Roman script in their own language and who therefore need a slow and methodical approach to learning to use the alphabet. If the exercises are unnecessary for your students, leave them out.

Activity 3.2

After studying page 26 together, students should be given time to explore their own dictionaries. Activity 3.2 may seem difficult, but students should work by elimination. They are only required to choose the correct headword, not to distinguish between different definitions under the same headword. **b** and **c** have numerical clues, and in **d** the sentence is similar to the example given in the dictionary.

Activity 3.4

If the students have different dictionaries, you can ask them to compare their answers and also to compare the different organisation of the dictionaries.

Unit 4

The purpose of this unit is to introduce students, in a fairly simple way, to textual reference and text organisation. The exercises here cannot, of course, be exhaustive, but they will serve to give students a start in a complex area which will be important in more advanced study.

Page 31 should be worked through with the students' books closed, and examples written on the board. Many students coming to English for the first time think that pronouns (and in particular *it*) refer to the first noun preceding them. Demonstrate that this is not always correct and that students must use the sense to help them. Start by putting two sentences on the board:

When I arrived at the school this morning, it was on fire.

When I arrived at the school this morning, it was 9 o'clock.

Ask what *it* refers to in each case. Explain that, in the second case, *it* is part of a fixed expression, and does not refer to anything. More complex explanations are not necessary at this stage.

Activity 4.2

First demonstrate this on the board.

Activity 4.3

Use the illustration to pre-teach *drum*.

Activity 4.4

Use the illustrations to pre-teach vocabulary.

Page 36 (conjunctions) should be worked through on the board, while the students' books are closed.

Activity 4.7

If the students are having problems, you can help them by giving them the first phrase of each part.

Unit 5

Students with a traditional educational background will be used to the idea that translation is an important way of dealing with a text in a foreign language. However, translation imposes upon the reader the notion that all parts of a text are of equal importance, and this contradicts many of the reading techniques that we adopt in our mother tongue. This unit introduces the student to two of these: skimming and scanning.

The introduction can be worked through with the students' books closed. The discussion should be very brief, and should take account of the fact that every person reads in a different way, and with different aims in mind. But there should be general agreement that some texts (eg guides, telephone bills) require the reader to search for specific information that he/she already has in mind; for others (film reviews, business letters) the reader looks for an opinion, perhaps, or the general idea (often called the gist). In some cases, the reader looks for fuller information – this will be dealt with in unit 6.

Activity 5.1

Make sure the students do not read the whole text before answering the questions (which they should do one at a time).

Activity 5.2

Some prediction exercises might be useful here: ask students for the names of some English towns, and what might be seen there. Again, make sure the students read the questions before looking at the text. You will find that students who are familiar with England will do this activity more quickly.

Activity 5.3

Do not pre-teach the vocabulary in the small ads. Some of it is very technical or specialist, and would not necessarily be comprehensible to a native-speaker. You may like to go through the vocabulary after the students have carried out the activity.

Activity 5.4

A follow-up activity might be to ask students which words and phrases helped them to decide on their answers.

Activity 5.5

To increase student motivation, put the students' ideas as to the gist of the article on the board before they read it, and then see who came closest to guessing it.

Unit 6

The aim of this unit is to give students practice in extracting most of the information from a text. In some cases, for example the information about cholera at the beginning of the unit, the readers will need to understand more or less every word, and so you may find it necessary to use dictionaries. Completing the activities without using dictionaries, however, may give the students a sense of achievement, and also help them to realise that it is often possible to understand something fairly fully without them. If you do decide to use dictionaries, make sure they are monolingual (see unit 3). In all the activities in this unit, it is recommended that the teacher spends some time introducing and explaining the activity (though preferably not pre-teaching vocabulary). Try not to let the students start the activities without preparation.

Unit 7

In this unit, students are given the chance to use different skills on slightly longer and more elaborate passages (four in all). The order of the exercises is not obligatory, but is probably the most logical.

Activity 7.1

Put the questions for the scanning activity on the board so that the students can see them before they read the text.

Activity 7.3

Prediction. Time spent on discussing the title and picture will be well rewarded. You might like to write students' ideas/predictions on the board, and (after an initial reading of the passage) tick off those which can be found in the passage.

Unit 8

Understanding a word from its context

You could introduce this unit by discussing with the students when and where it is not possible to use a dictionary.

Activity 8.1

Do this activity on an overhead projector, if possible, revealing one sentence at a time, to show how we build up our knowledge of a word by seeing it in different contexts. In this and the following activities, it is just as important to discuss with the students *how* they came to their conclusions as it is for the students to get the correct answers. In fact, mistakes can often be explored fruitfully, and a line of thinking which seems obvious to one student may not have occurred to another.

Activity 8.4

Before attempting this activity, students must be familiar with the following terms: *noun, adjective, adverb, verb, participle/–ing form, preposition.*

Activity 8.5

Once again, ask for justifications.

Activity 8.6

This is best done with an extrovert class. Group-work is recommended.

Understanding a word from its form

Other activities on word formation can be found in the sections on using monolingual dictionaries in unit 3. Introduce the section by writing the word *nation* on the board. Ask students for other words formed from it – e.g. *national, nationalist, nationalistic, international* (or use examples with *care, cook* and *life* from the book).

Comparative and superlative forms This is not intended to be a grammatical exposition, so make sure the students know this grammar point before starting the activity.

Word formation Students often say 'What does this word mean?' without realising that it derives from a word they already know. This activity is to awaken them to the possibility of using their previous lexical knowledge actively. Some explanation on the board may be useful before doing the activities.

Activity 8.11

Do not insist too much on grammatical accuracy in the definitions – the important thing is the *idea*.

Unit 9

For general comments on predicting, see the teacher's notes for unit 2.

Activity 9.2

This activity is designed to encourage students to use titles and sub-titles to predict what they will find in articles. You may like to ask students to supply more detailed predictions, such as the actual content.

Activity 9.4

An alternative might be to have the whole class put forward suggestions, which the teacher (or, better, one of the class) writes on the board. Those which in fact come up are ticked off.

Extra work on vocabulary etc should be done after the first reading, not before.

The rest of p. 75 – work through with students' books closed.

Activities 9.5/9.6

Group- or pair-work is recommended.

Activity 9.7

This is not intended as a gap-filling exercise, so make sure the students don't read ahead – either by using an overhead projector and revealing the text line by line, or by asking students to move a piece of paper down the page. Accept any logical answers.

Activities 9.8/9.9

See instructions for activity 9.7. Ask for justifications afterwards.

Unit 10

In this unit, students study some aspects of the dictionary in more detail. It is important for students to understand that in this way they are learning to use the dictionary and to help themselves with their studies of English in the future. They are not expected to learn how to use the words they study in this unit. They should however start to become familiar with the structure of English as this is a basic tool for further study.

It is recommended that the students work through the activities systematically from the beginning, as familiarity with the dictionary is important for the later exercises.

Activity 10.1

If students are familiar with basic grammatical concepts, this activity should cause no problems. For those who have never studied grammar, it may be necessary to expand the section by giving other examples and exercises.

Activity 10.3

Students should use this exercise to get to know their dictionaries. Many dictionaries contain a table of verbs, and this should be used to check their answers.

Activity 10.4

At this level, students should be aware of the large number of idioms and phrasal verbs in English. Explain that it is important to be able to understand them, but it is often not advisable to try and use them unless the student is completely sure of the correct context and register of the expression.

Unit 11

For general comments on textual reference, see the teacher's notes for unit 4.

This unit is divided into five parts (A-E) which deal with five of the problems students often encounter when reading, followed by some activities which combine the various problems. They are: A Contact clauses (no relative pronoun) B *this/that* C Elegant Variation D Conjunctions E *it*.

Students may have difficulty recognising that a problem exists at all, so each part starts with a problem sentence, which should be written on the board. The problem should be elicited from the students if possible, and then examples from this unit, and others devised by the teacher, can be given to clarify and explain the situation.

A It is extremely common in conversational English to omit the relative pronoun in defining relative clauses when the pronoun is the object of the relative clause. Students will encounter this when reading texts which include conversations (e.g. novels and short stories). (For a full explanation of the grammar of relative clauses, see Swan, *Practical English Usage* OUP.) Students are not required at this level to understand the fine points of the grammar involved, but only to be able to untangle what seems at first a baffling construction.

Work through the whole page of the first part of Section A on the board first, adding more examples as necessary.

Activity 11.1

It may be a good idea to work through questions 2 and 3 in open class first, to make sure all the students understand. Then continue in groups.

B and C You should work through the introductions with the whole class.

D Revise the simpler conjunctions *and*, *but* and *so* first, getting students to say when they are used, and asking for examples. Make three columns on the board – one each for *and*, *but* and *so*. These correspond to the columns in the book.

Explain that the conjunctions in column one (*also*, *as well as*, etc.) correspond in meaning (though not in grammar) to *and*, those in column two to *but* and those in column three to *so*. Take the students very carefully through the example sentences on page 89. It is not necessary for the purposes of the activity which follows for students to produce sentences with these conjunctions – it is more important that students understand the meaning of them.

Activity 11.4

The purpose of this activity is to encourage students to guess/estimate approximate meaning from context, using conjunctions. The students are not expected to write in the space the exact word they will see in the second sentence, but a word similar in meaning and appropriate in the context.

Do the first sentence as an example with the whole class. Make sure the students do not see sentence 1b before they write the word in the space in 1a. Then ask the students for their suggestions for the word in the space, and write them on the board – you should get words like *cold, wet, raining*. Now ask students to uncover the second sentence. They will probably have guessed a word which is similar in meaning to the word in sentence 1b.

E This section asks the students to discriminate between *it* as a pronoun, *it* as used in fixed expressions (such as *It's six o'clock*) and *it* as a preparatory subject. For full details, see Swan, op. cit.

Activity 11.5

Write the three example sentences on the board,

and keep them there during the activity for students to consult.

Activities 11.6/11.7

Use the illustrations to set up the exercises.

Activity 11.8

Make sure you discuss afterwards how the students came to their conclusions, and in particular which words in the text helped them to see how the story is organised.

Unit 12

For general remarks about skimming and scanning, see the teacher's notes for unit 5.

Activity 12.1

If possible, display a map of Scotland or of Great Britain to introduce this activity. When the students write their own questions for the scanning activity, you can either write all the questions produced by the class on the board, the answers to which they should then look for in the passage, or each individual student should look for the answers to his/her questions only. Either way, do not panic if only one or two of the answers can be found there – part of the skill of scanning is to find out if a text contains the information you need, or if it does not.

Activity 12.2

Make sure the students read the descriptions *before* reading the guide.

Activity 12.3

Weak classes should be asked to read the three summaries first. Explain difficult vocabulary in the summaries, but not in the articles: if you do work on the vocabulary in the articles, make sure it is after doing the main activity.

Activity 12.4

Ask students to justify their answers afterwards (they should be able to do this even if they have not understood everything in the text).

Activity 12.5

Explain what the gist is, how we often read articles quickly in our own language to find it (usually before deciding whether to read in detail or not) and how it can often be found in the first sentence or paragraph, and sometimes the last, of an article. There are no right answers to this activity, so accept any appropriate answers and encourage discussion.

Activity 12.6

This exercise practises both skimming and scanning. If a student or a pair of students finishes quickly, you can ask them actually to answer the questions on page 101.

Unit 13

Activity 13.1

This is a follow-up to activity 12.1. The first section ('Travelling around') is a scanning exercise. The students should look through the article quickly to answer the questions. The form-filling, however, requires more careful reading, and should be done after the students read the passage.

Once again, encourage students to do the activities without asking about, or looking up, difficult words. Any vocabulary work should be at the end.

Activity 13.2

The students should discuss the usual contents of a curriculum vitae before doing the exercise. You may wish to explain that the information provided does not come in the same order as the blanks on the c.v.

Activity 13.5

You may like to increase the predictive element in the students' reading by asking them to list the questions they would ask a famous writer if they had the chance; or by giving them the questions, and asking them to predict the answers.

Activity 13.6

This activity could be preceded by a class questionnaire, from which students find out which of their classmates have pets. The writing exercise should be done in groups.

Unit 14

Activity 14.1

Use the photograph to elicit some information about Budapest: that it is a (capital) city on a large river, etc.

Ask the students to read the four questions before reading the passage. Give them a time-limit for the first reading – perhaps a minute and a half. Then ask them to read the passage again more slowly, before doing the skimming and vocabulary-guessing activities which follow.

Activity 14.2

Use the title and illustration to get the students to predict some of the content of the article. The skimming must be done as quickly as possible. Then ask students to read the passage more carefully for the scanning, detailed information, and vocabulary exercises which follow.

Activity 14.3

As a pre-reading activity, ask students with glasses to take them off/put them on, and ask if they can *hear* better with the glasses on or off. Again, students should read the article quickly for the skimming activity, then more slowly for the other activities.

Activity 14.4

This activity is designed to increase the students' awareness of linking devices, so the discussion of the words which help in this is as important as the arranging of the sentences.

Activity 14.5

This activity is slightly different from the others. Explain to the students that most of the time when we read, we do not complete exercises on the piece: instead, we usually react by saying or thinking, 'Oh, that's interesting!' or, 'I didn't know that!' or, 'So what?'. The questions in this activity have no right or wrong answers – they are merely asked in order to provoke interest, and in one or two cases to predict what might come next. Teachers, however, should feel free to devise their own activities on the passage.

Key

Some activities have several possible answers, sometimes obvious: answers are not provided for these.

Unit 1

Activity 1.1: **1** e **2** h **3** g **4** f **5** b **6** a **7** d **8** c

Activity 1.2: **1** c **2** b **3** b **4** b **5** a **6** b **7** c **8** a

Activity 1.3: **1** c **2** b **3** a **4** a **5** c **6** c **7** b **8** a **9** b **10** a

Activity 1.4: 1) ski/skiing 2) water 3) books

Activity 1.6: *Across*: **2** job **4** town **5** wife **6** film
Down: **1** house **3** animal **7** meal

Activity 1.7: **1** e **2** g **3** h **4** f **5** c **6** b **7** d **8** a

Activity 1.9: **2** return ticket **3** sports centre, tennis match
4– **5** hotel bar **6** gas fire
7 fruit market
8– **9** photo shop, shop assistant
10 office use

Unit 2

Activity 2.1: **1** d **2** e **3** a **4** f **5** g **6** c **7** b

Activity 2.2: **1** f **2** e **3** a **4** b **5** c **6** d

Unit 3

Activity 3.1: (i) 1, 2, 3, 6, 8, 20, 23
(ii) 1, 5, 8, 9, 13, 14, 16, 20
(iii) 12, 13, 14, 16, 18, 19, 20
(iv) **a** beat, eat, feet, meat, sheet, wheat
b tall, tell, thin, time, top, tree, tunnel
c that, these, think, those, three, thug
d dark, deep, dine, dinner, eat, eight, electric, electricity, electronics, elephant, eleven

Activity 3.2: **b** 1 **c** 2 **d** 4 **e** 1

Activity 3.3: **b** 10 **c** 6 **d** 1 **e** 9 **f** 2 **g** 7 **h** 5 **i** 8

Activity 3.5: **1** pancake **2** tangerine **3** partridge
4 courgette **5** onion
6 oyster **7** cider
8 haddock **9** stuffing
10 chop

Unit 4

Activity 4.1: **2** Queen **3** shop assistant
4 beer **5** cats
6 supermarket **7** eggs
8 National Gallery
9 Hardiman
10 Lovitt Jeans
11 wine **12** Humber Bridge

Activity 4.2: **3** Refers to *Venice*
4 Fixed Exp.
5 Refers to *watch*
6 Fixed Exp.
7 Refers to *Peebles Hall*
8 Refers to *American pronunciation*

Activity 4.3: line 2 John line 3 drum
line 4 family line 5 drum/family
line 6 John line 7 drum
line 8 father line 9 John
line 10 drum line 11 Aunt Stephanie

Activity 4.4: a After that – 4   b Next – 3
c Finally – 5   d First – 1
e Then – 2

Order of pictures: 4, 3, 2, 5, 1.

Activity 4.5: Suggested order: 6 – 8 – 4
first type   2 – 7 second type
3 reasons for popularity
1 first   9 second   5 finally

Activity 4.6: 1 c   2 f   3 g   4 i   5 h
6 a   7 j   8 d   9 b
10 e

Activity 4.7: Part One 2 f   3 e   4 b   5 a
6 c

Part Two 2 e   3 a   4 c   5 f
6 d

Part Three 2 c   3 a   4 e   5 b
6 d

Unit 5

Activity 5.1: 1 £950   2 Includes 24th August, a bank holiday
3 swimming, tennis   4 No
5 £40   6 Yes   7 No
8 lunch Monday – Friday
9 a certificate   10 No

Activity 5.2: 1 a Cambridge   b Chichester
c Windsor   d Brighton
e Coventry   f Eastbourne
g Bath

2

	On the sea?	Castle?	Cathedral?	Roman?	Which London station?	Length of journey?
BATH	?	X	X	✓	Paddington	1 hour 15 mins.
BRIGHTON	✓	X	X	?	Victoria	58 mins
HASTINGS	✓	✓	X	?	Charing Cross	1 hr 45
SALISBURY	?	X	✓	?	Waterloo	1 hr 24
YORK	?	X	X	?	King's Cross	2 hr 10

Activity 5.3: 1 76666   2 9898 or 46700
3 668997   4 17 Dobson Avenue, London SE14
5 447790   6 788876

Activity 5.4: 1 a picnic   2 a record   3 a new book   4 a new computer   5 a volleyball match

Activity 5.6: 1 air hostess   2 nurse   3 lorry driver

Unit 6

Activity 6.1:

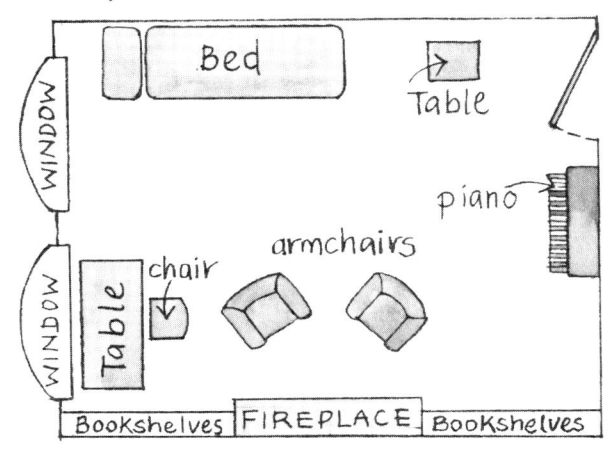

Activity 6.2:

	Quantity	Price Last Week	Price This Week
Apples	pound	44	46
Bananas	pound	52	52
Courgettes	pound	51	49
Mushrooms	¼ pound	23	33
Lamb Chops	pound	1.69	1.69
Beef	pound	2.52	2.46
Baked Beans	large can	28	26
Corn Flakes	large packet	83	85
Bread	large loaf	59	59
Total		£7.61	£7.65

Activity 6.3: A 1 Ken and Jackie   2 Mike
3 letter between friends
4 Ken and Jackie's visit to Bologna
B 1 T   2 F   3 T   4 F   5 T
6 F

Activity 6.4:

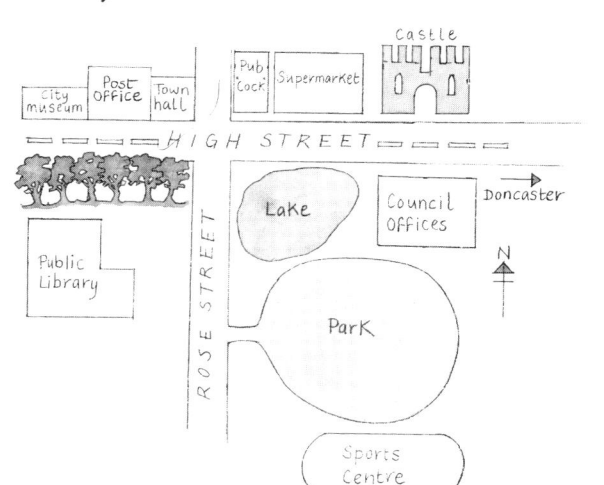

Activity 6.5:

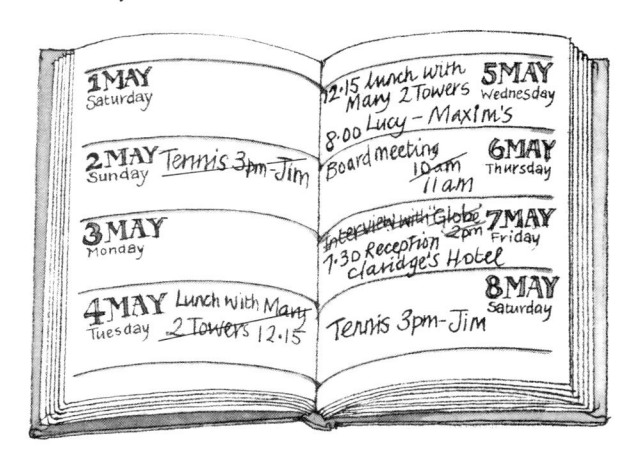

Activity 6.6:

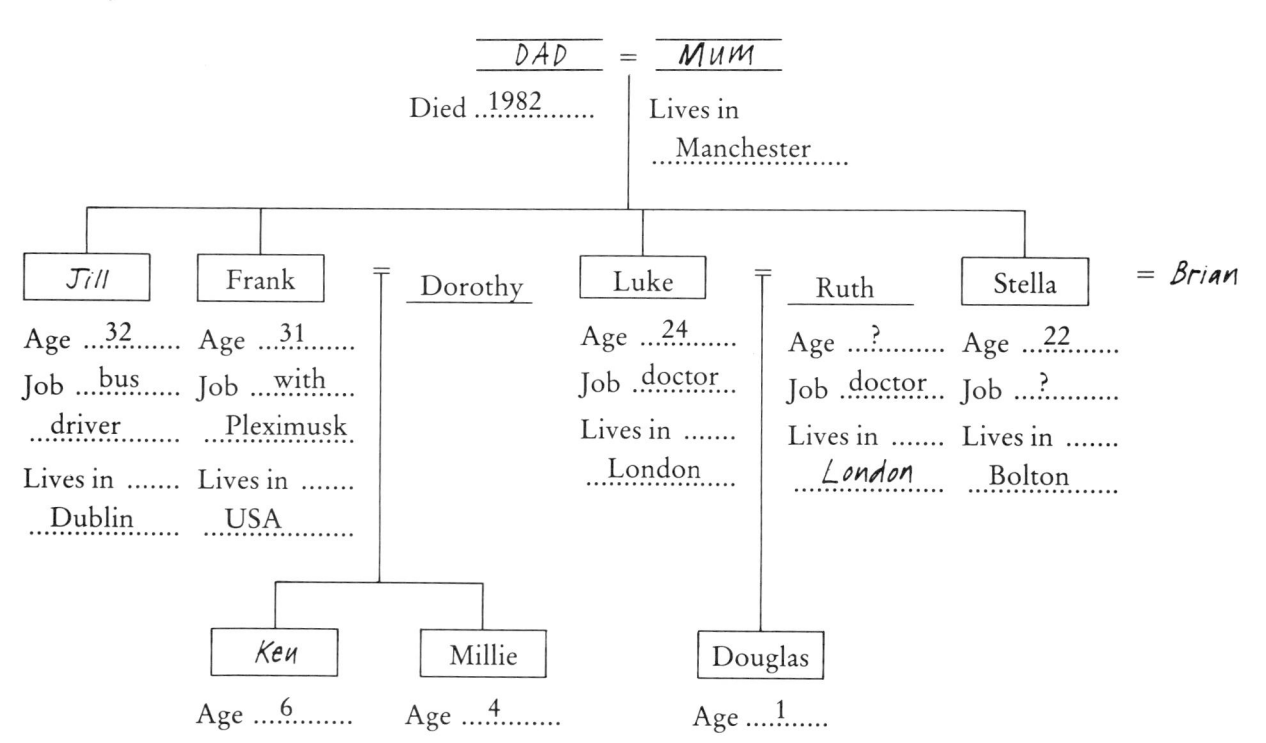

```
                    DAD  =  MUM
              Died  1982   Lives in
                           Manchester
```

Jill	Frank	Dorothy	Luke	Ruth	Stella = Brian
Age 32	Age 31		Age 24	Age ?	Age 22
Job bus driver	Job with Pleximusk		Job doctor	Job doctor	Job ?
Lives in Dublin	Lives in USA		Lives in London	Lives in London	Lives in Bolton

Ken — Age 6
Millie — Age 4
Douglas — Age 1

Activity 6.7:

BTB City Bus Tickets		
Name of ticket	How long does it last?	How much does it cost?
Tourist Ranger	2, 3 or 5 days	£4, £5.50 or £7.50
Monthly season	1 month	£26.50
Bus card	1 day	£2.50
Single ticket	1 journey	50p

	City Buses	Country Buses
Colour of buses?	orange	blue
Where do they operate?	all parts of the city	Conby, Rashville, Grill and villages in the area
Where do I buy tickets?	Post offices tobacconists BTB offices	on the bus
Minimum fare?	50p	75p
What time of day do services operate?	6.30 – 23.30	7.00 – 21.30
Where can I find timetables?	Bus stops	Bus stops

Unit 7

Activity 7.1: **A** 1 Mrs Anne Jones 2 cassette recorder
B a refund
C 1 a 2 b 3 a 4 b 5 b 6 b 7 a 8 b
D 2 T 3 T 4 F 5 F 6 F 7 F

Activity 7.2: **A** Students should tick the following: 1, 4, 5
B 1 24 September to 5 October 2 0232–75414 3 A

Activity 7.3: **B** Order of pictures: E – B – G – A – C – F – D
C 2 some friends and I 3 the sound 4 Frank 5 the old man 6 the choir 7 the sound
E 1 a 2 a 3 b 4 a 5 a 6 b

Activity 7.4: **A** 1 b 2 Sir Clough Williams-Ellis 3 9.30 am to 5.30 pm 1st April to 31st October

B 1 b 2 c 3 a 4 c 5 c 6 c 7 c 8 b
C 1 on the coast in North Wales 2 1925 3 rare plants and flowers 4 No 5 £1.70 6 where you can cook for yourself 7 Yes 8 books, gifts, jewellery, ladies' and children's fashions, antiques, Portmeirion pottery

Unit 8

Activity 8.2: 1 b 2 a 3 c 4 a 5 a

Activity 8.3: 1 film (Clues: darkness, seat, screen, woman with a torch, lights) 2 egg (Clues: shell, omelettes, cakes, pancakes, fried, scrambled, boiled, poached) 3 architecture (Clues: studied, buildings, design new buildings, church, cathedral)

Activity 8.4: 1 **a** noun **b** probably a kind of fruit
2 **a** -ing form of a verb **b** a physical activity such as climbing (following the pattern of *go skiing, go walking* etc.)
3 **a** adjectives **b** a physical description – something like *curly* or *brown*
4 **a** preposition **b** a word indicating position, like *by, near, on* etc.
5 **a** verb **b** *improved, declined, gone downhill* etc.
6 **a** adverb (of manner) **b** *carefully, quickly* etc.
7 **a** noun **b** job?
8 **a** noun **b** some kind of accommodation – *villa, hotel, chalet* etc.
9 **a** verb **b** *asked*
10 **a** adjective **b** a word describing physical or mental state – *ill, unwell, unhappy* etc.

Activity 8.5: *Across*: **1** doctor **3** mother **5** train **7** late **8** sleep **9** breakfast **10** stayed **11** sorry
Down: **2** tea **4** office **5** ticket **6** yesterday

Activity 8.7: **1** superlative adjective from *early* **2** noun **3** comparative adjective from *small* **4** noun **5** superlative adjective from *great* **6** noun **7** comparative adjective from *fat* **8** superlative adjective from *fast*

Activity 8.8: friend, office, sun, old, beautiful, toilet, warm, butter, hair, strong, poor, fire, famous, orange

Activity 8.9: **1** d **2** f **3** e **4** g **5** b **6** h **7** i **8** a **9** c

Activity 8.10: heart, know, hot, hungry, danger/dangerous, help, young, bored, rich, explain

Activity 8.11: **2** milk (Possible definition: 'with a lot of milk') **3** rain ('wet, with a lot of rain') **4** bicycle ('on bicycles, using bicycles') **5** furniture ('with furniture inside, provided with furniture')

Unit 9

Activity 9.1: **1** a **2** b **3** a **4** b **5** b **6** a **7** a **8** b **9** b

Activity 9.3: **a** 4 **b** 6 **c** 7 **d** 2 **e** 3 **f** 1/2 **g** 2 **h** 5 **i** 3/7 **j** 1 **k** 4 **l** 3

Unit 10

Activity 10.1: **3** n **4** v **5** v **6** n **7** n **8** v **9** v **10** n **11** n **12** v

Activity 10.2: Regular verbs: rush, await, milk, collect, harvest, plough, pick, help, create, solve
Irregular verbs: break, know, spend, learn, feed, send

Activity 10.5: **2** receive **3** cook **4** become **5** arrive **6** travel **7** catch **8** understand **9** find/hear/see **10** buy

Activity 10.6: **2** be careful **3** understand **4** stop **5** escape **6** discover **7** argue/quarrel **8** tolerate **9** die **10** happen

Unit 11

Activity 11.1: **2** *Main sentence*: The new car has broken down already. Which car? The car we've just bought
3 *Main sentence*: The story is called 'Cinderella'. Which story? The story I would like to tell you
4 *Main sentence*: The chair suddenly collapsed. Which chair? The chair he was sitting on
5 *Main sentence*: Let's go to that film. Which film? The film John was in
6 *Main sentence*: The glasses have been very useful. Which glasses? The glasses you gave us
7 *Main sentence*: The part of the city was near the castle. Which part of the city? The part of the city I was talking about
8 *Main sentence*: I saw the man the other day. Which man? The man you work with
9 *Main sentence*: The insect lives in Brazil and Ecuador. Which insect? The insect Robinson discovered
10 *Main sentence*: The novels were very sophisticated. Which novels? The novels Dickens wrote at the end of his life

Activity 11.2: **2** a **3** c **4** c **5** c **6** c **7** c **8** b **9** c

Activity 11.3: 2 husband; stupid man
3 hotel; building
4 Strathgorn; village; place; small community
5 Ethiopia, Mali, Mozambique; three countries
Africa; the continent
6 Roland Begel; President; leader
USA; great country; Queen of Democracies

Activity 11.5: 4 c 5 b 6 a 7 b 8 c,b 9 b

Activity 11.6:

Mrs Burningham was a strange character. She lived with her dog Timmy in a cottage in Putney. It was small and white, on the corner of Mansell Street and Common Road. She liked the house very much, I remember.

Her husband died in 1972 and Mrs Burningham was very sad – she loved him fondly – but she decided to stay in Putney. One day, about three years after this, her son and daughter-in-law came to see her. They came nearly every week, but there was something different this time. They brought some documents in a black briefcase, and wanted the old lady to look at them.

These documents gave the house to the children, and then Mrs Burningham could move into an old people's home nearby, which was very nice and comfortable, they said. But she didn't want to. She said it had a bad reputation.

Activity 11.7: **Line 5** Warmley **Line 6** cottage in Pelham Street **Line 8** the ghost **Line 10** Pelham Street **Line 10** Beth Mills **Line 12** the ghost **Line 14** the ghost **Line 16** Warmley **Line 17** ghost **Line 21** the other ghost **Line 23** Lion Hotel **Line 24** the waiter, Mr Patrick Slugg **Line 28** the hotel's owner, Mrs Gloria Honeycandle **Line 28–9** the other ghost **Line 30** the Lion Hotel

Activity 11.8: Part One 1 d 2 b 3 f 4 e 5 c 6 a

Part Two 1 d 2 f 3 b 4 e 5 a 6 c

Unit 12

Activity 12.2: Any reasonable suggestions accepted

Activity 12.3: 1 b 2 b 3 a

Activity 12.4: 1 b 2 a 3 b 4 b 5 c

Activity 12.6: 1 2 2 6 3 8 4 3 5 7 6 9 7 5 8 9 9 6 10 2

Unit 13

Activity 13.1:

1 Yes 2 Yes 3 From Caledonian MacBrayne, Western Ferries etc 4 Between Fort William and Mallaig.

TRAVELLING IN SCOTLAND
Main airlines operating in Scotland
<u>Air Ecosse</u>
<u>Loganair</u>
<u>British Airways</u>
Inclusive travel tickets:
a Highland Rover – operated by <u>British Airways</u> duration <u>14 days</u>
b Freedom of Scotland – operated by <u>British Rail</u> duration <u>7 or 14 days</u>
c Travelpass – Information from <u>Highlands and Islands Information Services</u>
Scenic railway lines:
Aberdeen – Inverness
Glasgow – <u>Stranraer</u>
<u>Glasgow</u> – Oban
<u>Perth</u> – Inverness
<u>Inverness</u> – Kyle of Lochalsh (Kyle Line)
For information on cruises and travel between islands, telephone (0475) 33755

Activity 13.2:

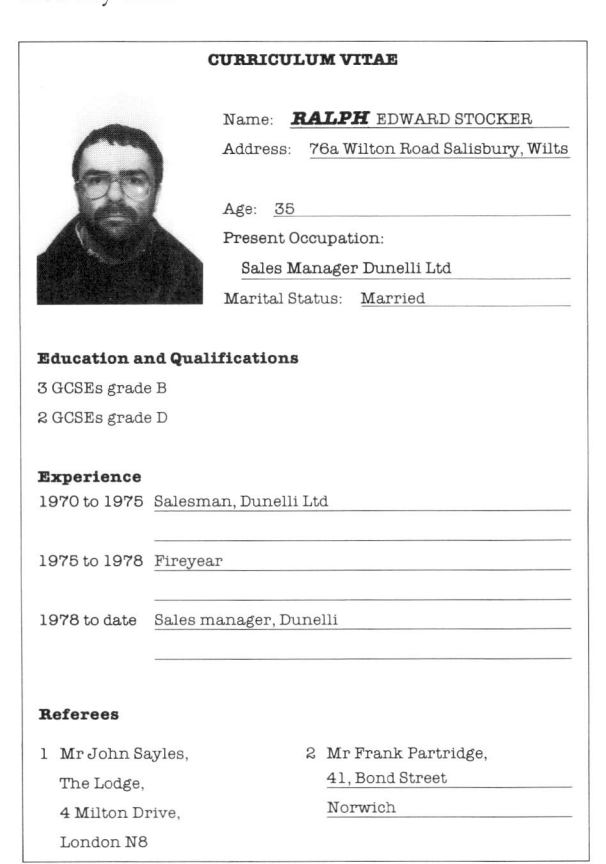

CURRICULUM VITAE

Name: **RALPH** EDWARD STOCKER
Address: 76a Wilton Road Salisbury, Wilts

Age: 35
Present Occupation: Sales Manager Dunelli Ltd
Marital Status: Married

Education and Qualifications
3 GCSEs grade B
2 GCSEs grade D

Experience
1970 to 1975   Salesman, Dunelli Ltd

1975 to 1978   Fireyear

1978 to date   Sales manager, Dunelli

Referees
1 Mr John Sayles,
   The Lodge,
   4 Milton Drive,
   London N8

2 Mr Frank Partridge,
   41, Bond Street
   Norwich

Activity 13.3:

(Seating arrangement around oval table: Kitchen side — Ulmar, Paul, Ralph Johnson; Window side; Mr Black on one end, Mrs Black on other end; Betty, Greta, Dennis Black)

Activity 13.4:

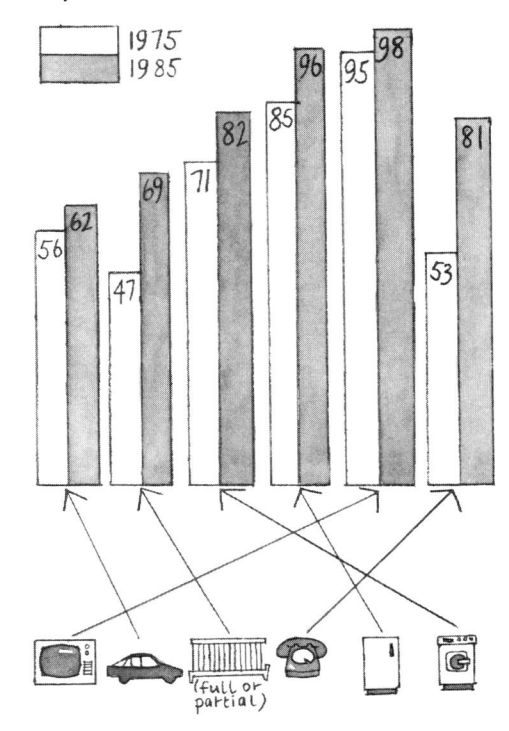

1975 / 1985

Bars: 56/62, 47/69, 71/82, 85/96, 95/98, 53/81
(items: microwave, car, central heating (full or partial), telephone, fridge, washing machine)

Activity 13.5:

the Editor
Peter Douglas

There were a number of errors in the article about Joanna Growles:

1. She hasn't lived here all her life.
2. She was at university in Newcastle.
3. "Pride" was published the year after she left school.
4. "Excessive Measures" was published in 1984.
5. She writes whenever she has the inspiration, at any time of day or night.
6. Her ex-husband lives in London.
7. "Overnight Success" is a play. Her eighth novel will be out next year.

Please put them right!

Activity 13.6:

A: 4 ✗	B: 12 ✓	C: 5 ✗
D: 2 ✗	E: 7 ✗	F: 1 ✓
G: 6 ✗	H: 3 ✗	I: 9 ✓

Unit 14

Activity 14.1: **A** 1 Hungary 2 Danube 3 2,064,307 4 summer
B 1 f 2 c 3 d 4 a 5 b 6 e
C 2 k 3 h 4 i 5 b 6 g 7 f 8 a 9 l 10 d

Activity 14.2: **B** 1 a thick cotton mattress 2 c
C 1 3″ or 6″ (inches) 2 Japan 3 Yes 4 £75–£95 5 Yes
D 1 Yes 2 No 3 Yes 4 No 5 Yes 6 No 7 Yes 8 Yes
E 2 k 3 g 4 a 5 j 6 b 7 h 8 c 9 d 10 f

Activity 14.3: **A** **Line 3** glasses **Line 13** the fact that you can hear better with your glasses on **Line 21** the fact that you can hear better with your glasses on **Line 27** reason **Line 31** eye and ear
B 1 a 2 b 3 a 4 a 5 a 6 a 7 b
C 1 You can hear better with your glasses on
2 Because you can lipread better with glasses; the frames of the glasses push your ears forward so you can hear more easily.
3 It happens on the phone too; it happens with contact lenses as well
4 The brain works harder with glasses off, so it spends less time on hearing; when we see well, we feel good about our other senses

Activity 14.4: **A** Correct order: See page 118
B **Line 3** the Andalusian town **Line 4** pm **Line 5** in the town square **Line 8** cafés **Line 8** it was the second part **Line 9** sad, they wanted to cry **Line 11** the experience **Line 11** our friends
C 1 a 2 b 3 b 4 a 5 a 6 b 7 a